Rosie

(and me)

Maui
March 19, 2019

Dear Nathan and John,
It is so nice to meet you. I hope you enjoy reading Rosie's story!
Love,
Carol

-a memoir-

Carol Harkavy

ROSIE *(and me)*

2nd Edition
ISBN   978-0-9988373-0-7

Harkavy, Carol 1. Mothers and daughters. 2. Parent-child relationship. 3. Inspiration. 4. Overcoming adversity. 5. Dealing with physical disabilities. 6. Reframing. 7. Bereavement. 8. Family. 9. Yiddish expressions. 10. New York 1920s-1950s.

website: rosieamemoir.wordpress.com
email: Rosie.memoir@yahoo.com

Rosie (and me) can be ordered at:
www.createspace.com/6275844

Reflections

For my husband Steve-
my hero and my greatest fan,
with love

GLOSSARY

bashert - meant to be; destined

farshtunkina - stinky; rotten

ketzila - little kitten (term of endearment toward a child)

loshon hora - gossip

macher - an important and influential person

S*habbos* - the sabbath (Saturday)

shidduch – arranged marriage

shlep - to pull with effort

tochter - daughter

tzaddik - a righteous person

yahrzeit - anniversary of a death

zindeleh - son

"We can complain because rose
bushes have thorns,
or
Rejoice because thorn bushes
have roses."

Abraham Lincoln

AUTHOR'S NOTE

"Death leaves a heartache no one can heal;
Love leaves a memory no one can steal"
                    Irish Proverb
            (taken from an old tombstone)

A huge part of my life is gone. Rosie is dead. My mother often said that no one is born a minute before their time or dies a minute after their time. Rosie's time came just past midnight on January 29, 2001, eighty-seven years, nine months, three weeks, and three days from the time she took her very first breath.

Even when I, myself, was a grandmother, I always felt that I was still attached to my mother by the umbilical cord! We were inexorably connected. I could read her thoughts as she did mine. We shared the same values and ideas; each loved our spouse and children unconditionally. Our lives were bound and intertwined in such a special way that her death has left a gaping hole in my heart.

This memoir is a tribute to a wonderful mother. It is her story as seen through the eyes of her baby.

Carol Harkavy

PROLOGUE

Brooklyn New York
June 24, 1944

We are getting ready for the wedding. Rosie is bustling around her apartment as quickly as a woman expecting a baby at any moment can. It is her oldest brother's wedding, and she does not want to be late.

When we get to the beautifully catered affair at the opulent Aperion Manor at 815 Kings Highway in Brooklyn, she greets her mother, Fanny, who turns to her neighbor and exclaims in a whispered voice, "That's Rosie - one of my two *farshtunkina tochters* (stinky daughters). The other one is over there. Frieda. Both of them married to poor shlubs - no money. At least Frieda's husband, Jack, accepted the kind offer of my sons to drive a truck for the feather factory. But Rose's husband, Simon. Not him. He was too proud. Told them to keep their crummy job. So what does he do? Cleans dirty clothes in his dry cleaning store. It will be the death of him. No wonder *Raisl* has the rheumatism. She should have listened to me and married Nathan Birnbaum. Such a successful accountant living in a magnificent apartment on Ocean Parkway instead of a walk-up in New York.

But did she listen? Of course not. But I must admit, her husband is better looking!"

Rosie overhears this exchange and sidles up to her sister Frieda.

"Too bad Papa isn't here," she sighs, tears welling up in her eyes. "He was so different from Mama. All Mama can talk about are her sons, her *zindelehs*. But Papa loved us just as much as the boys. Papa! How I miss you!"

"Papa" (Charles Geschwind), the patriarch of the family, is conspicuously absent. He was at work three years earlier when he died right in the arms of Manny, Rosie's baby brother, who was just fifteen. Morbidly obese, he dropped dead of a heart attack while tying his shoes. He was fifty-five years old.

Manny runs over to greet his oldest sister Rosie.

"Manny. So glad to see you. I can't believe you enlisted and leave next week to go into the army. I am so proud of you. Now that we have the real news about what the Nazis are up to in Europe, we need patriots like you to try to stop them. It was only a stroke of luck that Mama's cousin Itta and her daughter Stella got out. Maybe it was because they had blond hair and blue eyes that the woman guard in the concentration camp took pity on them and pushed them into the sewer to escape."

Rosie beams as she embraces the bridegroom, her older brother, Nat. He has recently returned from San Diego where he was an airplane mechanic in the United States

Army. She kisses Nat's newly betrothed wife, Evelyn, who could not look happier.

Rosie scans the room and spots her husband's sisters, Sarah and Sophie. Sarah, childless, rubs my mother's belly with a look of envy as Rosie winks at Sarah's husband Hymie, the lovable curmudgeon. Sophie, effusive and bubbly, always with a smile, rushes over, marveling that the baby has not yet arrived.

"Any moment now. Don't worry," she assures Rosie, as Sophie's husband, Abie, nods in agreement.

But Rosie isn't worried. In fact, she is the life of the party. With her radiant smile, rosy cheeks and big belly, she is the center of attention as she dances the Charleston from the 1920s, twirling around with her finger in the air and then wiggles to the newest craze, the rumba, followed by swinging to the music of the jitterbug, also known as the Lindy hop (named after Charles Lindberg's "hop" over the Atlantic Ocean). She grabs Frieda, and together they rip up the dance floor.

It is while dancing that I made a nuisance of myself and started kicking and carrying on, making it clear that we were not hanging around for dessert. I was ready to enter this world, and I could not be kept waiting!

We only had to go a little over a mile, a mere five minutes by cab to Madison Park Hospital, where we were supposed to meet Rosie's obstetrician, Dr. Michaelson, for what should have been a routine delivery. But he was either unavailable or unreachable, so we were literally in the hands of the intern on call that night. Unfortunately, he probably had not yet completed his obstetrics rotation, and because he was either too uncertain or too frightened to deliver a baby, he prevented a normal delivery by pushing my head in with his hand while my mother was desperately trying to push me out. The young intern was hoping that Dr. Michaelson would get to the hospital in time for the delivery so he forcibly held me back until the doctor's arrival.* When she realized what was happening, Rosie screamed at the intern, *"What are you doing? Do not harm my baby!"*

At that moment, Dr. Michaelson arrived and after assessing the situation, he gravely told my father, "The baby is gone. Pray for your wife."

But nothing would interfere with the welfare of her baby. My mother fought with all her strength to make sure that we both survived. Our lifelong bond, inadvertently strengthened by the hand of a frightened intern, was created at that very moment; and there was never a time thereafter that I would not have laid down my life for her nor she for me.

This was the beginning of a beautiful relationship upon which these memoirs are built.

---

*It was recently revealed that on September 13, 1918, an obstetrician was two hours late for the delivery of a baby to another mother named Rose. The nurse decided to prevent the birth by holding the baby's head inside the birth canal until the doctor's arrival. Deprived of oxygen, Rosemary Kennedy (President John F. Kennedy's oldest sister) probably suffered brain damage that negatively impacted her entire life.

PART ONE

THE BEGINNING

"*The best laid schemes (plans) of mice and men often go awry.*"

Robert Burns,
Poet (1786)

ONE

THE EARLY YEARS

"People make plans and God laughs."
(Old Jewish Proverb)

Two months after Congress ratified the 16th Amendment to the Constitution establishing a federal income tax and two weeks after New York City opened its first skyscraper (the Woolworth Building) Rosie was born on April 5, 1913, in Brooklyn, New York, the second oldest of eight children, consisting of five boys and three girls (one of whom, Chana, died at the age of two). Her parents were sixteen when a *shidduch* (arranged marriage) was made for them. Ongoing anti-semitism was second only to conscription into the army as motivation for leaving Mielec.*

*The thriving Jewish presence in Mielec dwindled as anti-semitism pervaded the town. Subsequently in 1939, on the eve of Rosh Hashanah (the Jewish New Year), the Nazi occupiers of Mielec shot or burned alive Jews they pulled naked from the *mikvah* (ritual bath). These atrocities persisted, culminating on March 9, 1942, when as a final blow, the Nazi monsters transformed the town into a concentration camp. (Details on the history of Mielec can be found in *Mielec, Poland – The Shtetl That Became a Nazi Concentration Camp* by Rochelle G. Saidel.)

1

In order to spare his son the cruelty meted out by the Czar's army aimed at stripping conscripts of their Jewish identity, my great-grandfather paid off a government official to allow my grandparents to leave Poland and emigrate to France in 1903. Seven years later, they boarded the *RMS Majestic* (the precursor to the White Star Line's *RMS Titanic*) and made their way to America where they settled on Rivington Street on the Lower East Side of New York City.

Fanny, Rosie's mother, was a strong, domineering businesswoman, who cherished her sons and barely tolerated her two surviving daughters. She acted upon this favoritism toward her sons by leaving her entire fortune to them and one dollar to each of her daughters. This was specified in her will so that neither daughter could claim that the absence of an inheritance to the females was an oversight!

Rosie's father, Charles, was the complete opposite of his wife. His kindness, generosity and sweet personality were all passed on to Rosie. He was honest and trusting, loyal and caring, earning the reputation among his peers of being a *tzaddik* - a righteous person. Given this title, he was regarded as someone more like an angel than a human being, and, on top of that, the most human of human beings, always doing what was correct and just, ever striving to make everything the way it should be. Rosie encompassed the strength of her mother and the kindness of her father.

Rosie came of age in the roaring 1920s. Years later, her friends would tell me that she was the liveliest, smartest, and most energetic of their entire group. She danced the Charleston while shimmying her slender body, immersed herself in her schoolwork often pounding the keys of her Olivetti typewriter late into the night, and she was always game to hop on the "D" train to Coney Island for a Nathan's hot dog. An honor student at James Madison High School, her plan was to go on to Hunter College and pursue her dream of becoming a teacher. Her wealthy parents could easily afford her college education. It was 1929. Her lofty plans were dashed when the stock market crashed and people who lost everything jumped out of windows. Her father's business plummeted. College was out of the question, and she had to go to work to help support the family.

She changed gears seamlessly and without complaints. Even during her early years, she adjusted to her new reality - the first of many adjustments she would have to make throughout her life - a chameleon who adapted to whatever obstacles stood in her way.

TWO

THE LOVE STORY

Swan Lake, 1934

She is standing at the shore of the magnificent lake dotted with small summer resorts beyond which rise the majestic Catskill Mountains, three-and-a-half hours by bus from her parents' home in Brooklyn. She and her girl-friend are escaping from the sweltering New York City summer heat by sojourning up to the Mountains for a short vacation - for some cool fresh country air, some rest and relaxation. She is twenty-one years old, slim, erect, beautiful, and filled with life and enthusiasm. She has described the scene to me so often that I can picture it vividly in my mind. It is a perfect summer day, cool and sunny. She sees a handsome young man rowing a boat on the lake. So in awe of him, she tells her friend, "See that man. That's the man I'm going to marry!" Her friend laughs and reminds my mother that she is already en-gaged to a promising young accountant hand-picked by her domineering, wealthy mother, but she doesn't care. *This* was the man she would marry.

He, too, had gone to the country to escape the oppressive New York City heat. He and his widowed mother had left behind their Lower East Side tenement and serendipitously ended up in Swan Lake.

The fact that their paths crossed at all was nothing short of a miracle. Their lives were on two parallel tracks with no chance of meeting, except that they did at an unexpected junction called Swan Lake.

Simon grew up in a tenement on Clinton Street on the Lower East Side of Manhattan, where the toilet was in the yard and there was no central heat. His widowed mother brought him and his siblings to America when he was three, right after her forty-one-year-old husband died in Austria. Because she could not leave her toddler home alone while she worked in a sweat shop and her other children went to school, she immediately registered him in kindergarten, telling the authorities that he was the required age of four. Actually born in 1910, his New York City school record shows 1909, the year his mother told the principal at P. S. 120 so he would be old enough to register. No birth certificate was expected from a poor immigrant from Eastern Europe.

Rosie, on the other hand, was born in America to a wealthy family and enjoyed a privileged life, residing in an opulent apartment on South Ninth Street in Williamsburg, Brooklyn. When her family came to America, they lived on Rivington Street, just ten blocks away from Clinton Street. But they had moved up into Brooklyn and now considered the Lower East Side beneath them, leaving it behind for the greenhorns and the gentiles. The Geschwinds preferred to live in their Jewish upper class enclave in Brooklyn.

How Simon and Rose landed at the same small resort in Swan Lake is a mystery. Some would say that it was *bashert* (God's plan and meant to be). There is no other explanation.

I can picture how their first encounter played out. She, outgoing and lively, approached him after he finished rowing, while he, more reserved, was only too happy to be greeted by such a beautiful young woman. I picture them walking, running, hiking, dancing, and rowing, all the while filled with excitement and merriment, their hearts bursting with the euphoria of young love. She is free of pain with straight, strong fingers and slim but muscular legs, innocent and ignorant of the pain she would encounter just seven years later and which would plague her for the rest of her life.

* * * * *

Their love story continued, and on April 6, 1935, the day after her twenty-second birthday, my mother married the love of her life. They were married in the synagogue where her father was a big *macher* (important person) surrounded by two hundred and fifty guests, all there to celebrate the marriage of Charles Geschwind's eldest daughter to Simon Anderman, a poor, albeit handsome, young man from the Lower East Side. She looks stunning in a silk lace gown that hugs her slender body, carrying a bouquet of calla lilies, while he is striking in his white bow-tie and tails. They are very happy as they start their life together in a small Brooklyn apartment, while my father struggles to earn a living as a delivery boy in a cleaning store.

PART TWO

LIFE INTERFERES WITH LIFE

"Face your deficiencies and acknowledge them; but do not let them master you.
Let them teach you patience, sweetness, insight."

Helen Keller

ONE

ADVERSITY

"Accept whatever comes and meet it with courage and the best you have to give."

Eleanor Roosevelt

It started slowly, insidiously, with minor pains in her hands and feet. Reluctantly, she went to a doctor who told her that there was nothing really wrong with her, and, like so many young wives, all she wanted was her husband's attention. Embarrassed by what this misogynist told her, the naive twenty-eight-year-old did not question his diagnosis, and she tried to ignore the disease that was to eventually consume her body. A year later, when the pain had escalated, she saw another physician who made the correct diagnosis of psoriatic rheumatoid arthritis. "How sad," this sympathetic doctor said. "An old woman's disease at such a young age."

She tried all the new treatments that were available at the time, but nothing seemed to work. She tried gold injections and rest and was advised to expose her psoriasis-ridden painful body to ultraviolet light. I can recall the violet-blue rays emanating from the sunlamp and the small oval-shaped white goggles that my mother wore to protect her eyes. I imagine that her eventual blindness fifty years later from macular degeneration can be traced to this aggressive treatment for her arthritis.

How clearly I remember as a small child when we lived in a brownstone railroad flat on Sixteenth Street in New York City, seeing my mother's thumbs so different from those of my friends' mothers. They arched back very far, "on their own," I thought. I couldn't understand why. After all, smiling, she would call to me, "Come here, *Ketzila* (little kitten)", as she plugged in the curling iron with the black and white speckled cotton cord and the green wooden handle to put Shirley Temple curls into my stick straight hair. It could not have been easy on her painful fingers that seemed to effortlessly maneuver the gadget to curl my hair without scorching it.

After repeatedly ripping the hems of my dresses while playing with the blocks on the floor in kindergarten, I tried desperately to explain to my mother that when I stood up, the heel of my shoes got stuck in the hem, ripping the fabric. "That's okay, *Ketzila.* Don't worry," she would smile, as she made the repairs with the precision of a "blind-stitch" (hemming) machine, never getting annoyed at my carelessness.

She taught my sister and me how to crochet and proudly displayed the intricate, ornate doilies she herself made when her fingers were more nimble and limber. I wonder if she knew that the crocheted squares placed on the backs of chairs were called "antimacassars" and were originally designed to protect the fabric from the macassar hair cream that men used in the 1850s to smooth down messy hair.

We certainly kept my mother busy. Once, while crossing Fourteenth Street with four lanes of cars, trucks, and buses, I ran out of my carriage directly into the traffic. The behavior of my older siblings was not exemplary that day either. Rosie, the disciplinarian of the household, held the philosophy that even if only one of us was misbehaving, we all were punished. So, after we reached the other side of Fourteenth Street in one piece, she walked us into the Five and Ten Cents Store (hitherto the source of our delicious treats, *Charlotte Russes* - a white cupcake piled high with whipped cream and a cherry on the top housed in a white cardboard cup) and asked to speak to the store manager. No *Charlotte Russes* for us that day! She asked the manager if he had a cat-o'-nine tails. She meant to frighten us so we would never run out into the street again, but none of us had a clue as to what a cat-o'-nine tails was so the lesson was completely lost on us. Had we known that she was asking for a whip with nine knotted cords attached to it for the purpose of beating us, we might have paid more attention! The manager was not amused and, not realizing that she asked for this in jest, threatened to report her to the Society for the Prevention of Cruelty to Children. My poor mother rushed out of the store, not with a cat-o'-nine tails but with her tail between her legs and a sheepish smile on her lips, as the manager looked at her with scorn and at us three little darlings with great pity, while his hand rested on the telephone debating whether or not to report her to the authorities.

Nothing seemed to abate the pain of my mother's rheumatoid arthritis, and nothing prevented its acceleration - not the sixteen aspirins a day, not the hot paraffin wax treatments, not the application of Oil of Wintergreen, or the ultraviolet lamp treatments. So, in 1955, at the still young age of forty-two, when a dentist told her that the poisons of the arthritis ravaging her body were concentrated in the teeth and gums and that extracting her teeth could offer relief, Rosie, in utter desperation, had all her teeth pulled. We had just moved to Spring Valley, New York, a small town thirty-five miles north of New York City. How vividly I remember as a young child of ten coming home from school, getting off the school bus, letting myself into the house, and going up the steep flight of stairs to my mother's bedroom at the end of the hall where she was lying in her bed surrounded by wads of bloody tissues. I clearly recall feeling such sadness and helplessness combined with inexplicable fear and uncertainty of what this new seemingly powerless mother would be like - less strong, less in control, more vulnerable, more skeptical. It wasn't for another decade that I would learn Freud's interpretation that dreaming about teeth falling out was a sign of insecurity.

Not only did this barbaric treatment not eradicate Rosie's arthritis, it created a new problem and source of pain that she never had before. She developed blisters in her mouth and gums from false teeth that never seemed to fit, making and remaking set after set, until it became obvious that a comfortable set of false teeth was not in the cards.

She wore sturdy lace-up, low stacked heels (old lady shoes for a young woman with an old-lady's disease) and then resorted to wearing clumsy Murray Space shoes molded to fit her progressively misshapen feet.

In 1963, she went to the Leon N. Levi Hospital in Hot Springs, Arkansas, where she was taught proper diet and exercise as she immersed herself in the hot springs to help alleviate some of the painful effects of her crippling disease. She returned home and tried to replicate the routine she followed at the hospital, buying a juicer and drinking fresh carrot and spinach juice, placing her hands in hot paraffin wax and keeping the wax on until it congealed over her painful fingers and joints. But the disease, which for some eventually goes into remission or burns itself out, never abated. Her psoriasis became progressively worse. She wore long sleeves, winter and summer, retaining her dignity and modesty by not allowing others to see the sores and scabs from her elbows to her wrists.

* * * * *

Until his death in 1984, my father had been Rosie's greatest advocate and probably the reason she retained her independence for so long. Despite her pain, he made her walk.

"Come on, Rosie. Let's get going. Remember what they told you in the hospital. 'Stomach in! Tits out!'"

And with great effort to straighten her shoulders and lift herself out of her chair, she would smile, "What can I do? He's my sweetheart. How can I disappoint my *Shimshee?*"

A spry, athletic, trim, energetic man, my father never complained about the compromises in his life as a result of his wife's debilitating disease. He had taken his marriage vows seriously, and he stuck by her in sickness and in health, in good times and in bad. He reinforced her mental strength and her emotional stamina, while maximizing whatever physical capabilities she still had. But it was not a one-way street. In return, she offered him peaceful advice, endless encouragement, and calm reaction to otherwise calamitous events. His physical stamina combined with her mental fortitude melded into a single embodiment stronger than either could have achieved without the other.

TWO

ADJUSTMENTS

*"Resolve to keep happy,
and your joy and you shall form
an invincible host against difficulties."*

Helen Keller

Rosie was a master at reframing. To reframe is to take one's thoughts regarding an otherwise adverse situation and turn them into something positive. Even when she could no longer see the expressions on her loved ones' faces, she rejoiced in embracing and kissing them or talking to them on the telephone. Unable to walk, she vicariously shared the excitement of her grandchildren when they told her about their skiing in Lake Tahoe, dancing at a bar mitzvah, or hiking in the Ramapo Mountains. Severe pain in her joints did not embitter her nor did it diminish the joy she got from knowing that her family loved her and valued her opinions. Rosie had a multitude of ailments, any one of which would have driven most people into severe depression and self-pity, but she concentrated on the good in her life, not the bad.

Her magical ability to reframe was apparent long before her physical decline. The oldest girl in a family with seven siblings, my mother loved children and her dream was to become a teacher. I can picture her, a bubbly happy high school student, member of the first graduating class of James Madison High School in her native Brooklyn, New York, eagerly looking forward to attending Hunter College and fulfilling her dream of becoming a schoolteacher. The inscription beside her name in the 1930 edition of *The Log*, her high school yearbook, indicates that she was a member of the Madrigal club (the school choir which, based on her love of singing but inability to carry a tune, took a lot of courage to join!), the current events club, the Student Council, and Maxwell Teachers Training program. The ditty below her picture says: "She's a noisy miss and never on time; That's not the truth, but helps our rhyme."

There was no question that she would be admitted to Hunter despite the stringent academic requirements for acceptance at what was then the premier public college in New York City - the sister school of City College which was dubbed "the poor man's Harvard." Her ambition and enthusiasm were second only to her excellent scholastic record reflected in part by her prized silver medal "for excellence in mathematics" which she treasured all her life. Even when her dreams of becoming a teacher were crushed because of the Great Depression, requiring her to join the work force instead of the college community, she reframed. A perfectionist, she became a happy and successful legal secretary, but her lifelong dream was never forgotten.

She eventually fulfilled her own dream vicariously through her children. She insisted that we all get a teaching license. My sister Pearl taught second grade and eventually owned and operated a nursery school; my brother Siggy taught at a 600 school for delinquent youths in New York City; and I taught at The City College of New York.

PART THREE

THE CUP IS HALF FULL

*"Most folks are about as happy
as they make up their minds to be."*

Abraham Lincoln

ONE

ROSIE, THE OPTIMIST

"Never give in. Never. Never. Never."

Winston Churchill

New York City

Refusing to surrender to an "old woman's disease," she stares fate in the eye and dares it to rob her of life's joy. We walk to our violin lessons on Greenwich Street in Greenwich Village in New York City while she balances two violins, one in each hand, stopping on the way back to watch young girls jumping rope to "Double Dutch." She takes the ropes at one end and expertly turns them in opposite directions with the precision of a cowboy whirling his lasso at a rodeo. Then, with five blocks to go until we reach home, she takes us to Mabel's Candy Store, catty-cornered at the intersection of Seventh Avenue and Eighth Street, where we share a chocolate malted served in white cone cups securely placed in shiny chrome holders. While we spin on leather upholstered fountain stools, Mabel, the gray-haired proprietor, complains that a Hershey bar is going up a penny to six cents.

She draws a hop-scotch game with chalk on the sidewalk and demonstrates how to carefully throw a stone or a bobby pin onto a number and then hop on one foot until reaching the end where you land on both feet and jump around hopping back to the stone, bending down balanced on one leg, picking up the stone or bobby pin and jumping off the hop-scotch board. With a "who-knows?" shrug and a twinkle in her eye, she informs us, "Don't ask me why, but here in New York, we call the game 'potsy'."

She squeezes fresh orange juice every morning by hand, fills our Howdy-Doody and Cinderella lunch boxes with cream cheese and jelly sandwiches, an apple, and a thermos of milk. She washes the clothes and stands on the fire escape with a bag of clothespins pinching each one with her already deformed fingers, painful I am sure, but never letting on. Later, she irons and folds the clothes to the perfection they had when newly purchased, scrubs the sinks and tubs with Ajax, mops the floors with CN, a brown disinfectant whose distinct odor alone could kill any germ it touches, and dusts all of the furniture with Old English scratch remover polish to such a sheen that an unexpected visitor once marveled at the spotlessness of the railroad flat apartment, remarking that "you could eat off the floor."

Spring Valley, New York

They give up everything in New York City, and when he expresses any doubt in their decision, Rosie reminds my father that in 1927, she wrote in her autograph album that her favorite hero was the naturalist, John Burroughs, who said: "Leap and a net will appear." So they take a leap of faith, and in 1955, they sell their cleaning store in New York City and buy a dilapidated old rooming house in Spring Valley. Rosie helps my father renovate the place, clinging to the memory of her more energetic days when enthusiasm was all that was necessary to keep her going, when she was not encumbered by the pain and limitations of her diseased body. She paints a large sign ANDERMAN'S BUNGALOWS and helps to transform the uninhabitable rooms into comfortable summer apartments to bring in an income. My father, the maverick who stole my mother's heart so many years before, sold *Mack Quality Cleaners*, his cleaning store on the corner of Fourteenth Street and Seventh Avenue - his only means of support - and moved his entire family to the old rooming house on six acres in Spring Valley that he purchased with his life's savings of sixteen thousand dollars. In our 1954 Kaiser sedan, we follow the rickety moving truck, without a name, that is overflowing with all our worldly belongings. I spot our twelve-inch black-and-white television set, hoping that our prized possession would not fall out of the truck and break during the journey. It could have been a scene from the "Beverly Hillbillies" that would air decades later.

She relinquishes city life with no regrets and proudly slips into her new role as country wife, marveling, "Who would have guessed that Rosie would be married to a city boy turned country squire." Together they oversee their six-acre "estate," one acre of which is dotted with the remaining trees of a long-forgotten apple orchard from which we salvage the partially rotten apples that have fallen from the neglected trees. Most of the apples are inedible, but Rosie manages to cut away the worm holes and soft spots and then cook them into a delicious applesauce using the same vintage Foley mill she uses to make soup from my father's tomato crop. His garden is meticulously planted in rows of corn, peppers, string beans, and rhubarb. She cuts off the poisonous leaves of the rhubarb, noticing how shiny the saucepan becomes after she cooks the stalks - so whenever her pots are dull, she decides to cook rhubarb! Little did she know that it was the oxalic acid in the rhubarb that made her pots shine.

Together, they design their version of a chicken coop, using wire to surround the abandoned outhouse with the crescent moon cut-out on top that is still standing on the property. We gather enough eggs so "eggs" is no longer added to the grocery list. When we aren't gathering eggs, Rosie commands us to "Go pick some rocks" to keep us occupied during her afternoon naps. She says it in the same intonation and syntax as if she is telling us to "Go pick some flowers" or "Go pick some berries!" We take this job very seriously because it is not merely an exercise in futility to keep us busy. My father uses the small rocks to reinforce the cement he mixes in his miniature cement mixer and then pours to lay a sidewalk or build a porch.

With great anticipation, she opens a small dress shop that she proudly names *Anderman Apparel,* joining *King Kotten* and *Betty's Corset Shop* on Main Street, where she painstakingly and painfully wraps the thirty-nine-cent neckerchief and fifty-nine-cent kerchief in a box with colorful paper and ribbons that she curls using the edge of a pair of scissors. I meet her there after school and help as much as an eleven-year-old can. The store fails - the most expensive item is a dress for $6.98; and my parents put all of their efforts into converting the rooming house into small apartments to be rented on a weekly basis to transients who are newly divorced, alcoholics, or just down on their luck.

She enrolls in the local community college and registers for English and Psychology classes, where she wows her professors and young classmates with her insights on family and love. The psychology professor gives her an A-plus on her essay describing the different kinds of love: the romantic love for a spouse, the nurturing love for a child, and the reverent love for a parent. He marvels that his introductory course is the first class in psychology she has ever taken and compliments her on her enormous insight, stating that her explanation of human nature rivals explanations given in most textbooks.

At fifty-three, she learns how to drive, and after knocking down the cones placed there to guide her in the parallel parking segment of her driver's test, she charms the officer who gives her the test, promising that she will never parallel park, and he passes her! *"See, Rosie, it's true!"* she says to herself. *"You **do** catch more flies with honey than with vinegar!"*

She shops for groceries and exercises at Jack La-Lanne, always driving home on the exact same route so that my father can find her in case she doesn't make it home.

Waldwick, New Jersey

In 1983, Rosie has her arthritic hip and knee replaced simultaneously and, while recovering from her surgeries, my father is diagnosed with acute leukemia. Unable to manage in their large house in Spring Valley, I move them to a condo at Tamaron in Waldwick, New Jersey, three miles away from me. It is great having them nearby. The following year, my father dies, leaving Rosie a widow at seventy-one.

The new friends they made at Tamaron watch out for Rosie, and she meets Harry, a new resident whose wife dies two weeks after he moves in. Together, they take a "dry run" to the baseball field where my ten-year-old Emily plays baseball for Little League. They want to make sure they know the route when she has a practice or a game.

Determined to enjoy life to its fullest, she signs up for the talent show at the clubhouse of her condominium at the age of seventy-eight and lip-sings Barbra Streisand's "Second Hand Rose," shuffling her feet and smiling from ear to ear, while holding her friend Harry's hand for support.

She plays pinochle and gin rummy, poker and blackjack, warning us never to play with strangers, reminding us how her father got swindled by a bunch of card sharks returning home on an ocean liner after buying feathers in Europe for his pillow factory in Brooklyn. In her old age, she takes the bus to the casinos in Atlantic City with the other senior citizens and stops only when her vision has failed her and she is confined to a wheelchair.

At eighty-five, she fulfills a lifelong promise and prepares for a trip to California for her oldest granddaughter's wedding, bringing along her wheelchair, commode, dignity diapers, breathing machine, and seven different medications.

* * * * *

"So, Rosie, how do you do it?" I laughingly ask after she tells me that she picked two winning lottery numbers. She answers me as seriously as if she were responding to a philosophical question on how she is able to maintain such emotional and mental fortitude in the midst of such physical decline. Sitting in her wheelchair, looking down as if contemplating a complicated mathematical problem, she lifts her fragile misshaped index finger to her temple and answers, *"I just do."*

Long before email, Twitter, and Facebook, she was the social network for the goings-on of the entire family. She knew what was happening in Los Angeles, San Francisco, Albany, New York City, Florida, Teaneck, and Baltimore.

She took special delight in sharing with her grandchildren the insights she had gleaned from nearly a century of life. They realized the treasure they had, and their relationship with their Grandma strengthened as they approached the summers of their lives while she was entrenched in the winter of hers. A gap of sixty years, spanning three generations, did not diminish the impact she had on her grandchildren. Whether it was a discussion on Torah law or corporate law, on being an entrepreneur or an editor, on aspiring to become a film-maker or a homemaker, on the trials and tribulations of starting a business or a family, on career-building or child-rearing, her ideas were always on target and well-received.

Her optimism was evident everywhere. She would say that her grandchildren's dirty diapers *"smelled like perfume!"* and even put an optimistic spin on fairy tales that were notoriously dark.

"Grandma, I like your stories the best. They always have happy endings when *you* tell them to me!"

It was true. She Disneyfied the most gruesome fairy tales. Hansel and Gretel made it home safely; the big bad wolf never ate Little Red Riding Hood's grandma; the three little kittens didn't lose their mittens; and the three little pigs were safe in their makeshift houses. Everyone lived happily ever after. Rosie was determined to do the same. No matter what hardships befell her, she would be happy.

Kind and sweet as she was, Rosie was no pushover. Even though she was a very good card player, when Rosie played cards with her grandchildren, she always let them win. One time, after letting her oldest granddaughter win over and over again at gin rummy, the eight-year-old told her, "Grandma. You should sleep with the cards under your pillow so you will learn how to play better!" That was the last time Elissa beat Rosie at gin rummy!

31

TWO

ROSIE, THE SMILER

"The robbed that smiles, steals something from the thief."

William Shakespeare
(Othello)

Bravery and wisdom, strength of character and of mind, and physical suffering that was accompanied with a positive attitude all were intertwined with her unique sense of humor. Sitting in her wheelchair at the dining room table, the telephone within reach, Rosie was in her favorite place, waiting to receive calls or making them. Emma, her home-health aide, was expecting a call from her bookie (to whom she owed money) and had given Rosie strict orders to tell anyone who called for her that she was not there. So when the telephone rang, my mother picked up the receiver with her warm "Hello" followed by "Who's this?" "Oh!" And as she mouthed the name of her bookie, Emma who was standing next to my mother, shook her head vigorously and mouthed back,

"No. Tell him I'm not here!" So my mother, very professionally said, "Oh, Emma? She's not here right now. Can I take a message?" While Rosie was dodging the call so adroitly with Emma right in front of her, she was nearly hysterical with pent-up laughter, her eyes tearing and her smiling mouth barely able to form the words needed to convince the caller that Emma, indeed, was not there. The incredible part of it all was that she was looking straight at Emma the entire time!

She never showed the humor that would leave people reeling with laughter or slapping their knees. Hers was more a gentle sense of what would make people happy and smile, not necessarily what would make them laugh. I know that I get my emphasis on smiling from my mother. She encouraged us to join her while she sang the World War II tune that John Gambling played on WOR radio every morning:

"Pack up your troubles in your old kit pack
and smile, smile, smile.
What's the use of worrying?
It never was worthwhile.
So pack up your troubles in your old kit pack
and smile, smile, smile!"

THREE

ROSIE, THE MILLIONAIRE

"I have four million dollars," she brags to her freshman English composition class at Rockland Community College. At fifty-five years old, she is old enough to be the grandmother of her classmates and probably twice the age of her professor. Her audience looks at her wide-eyed and envious.

"Wow!" cries out one young student. "Can I float a loan?" he jokes.

The teacher, more reserved, asks, "How did you become so rich?"

"Was it the lottery?" a hopeful young *ingenue* asks.

Rosie just smiles, and with a twinkle in her eye, confesses.

"Actually, I am not rich at all - not in monetary terms, anyway. But I have four million dollars. I have my husband, that's one million; and a million for each of my three children. And there you have it - four million dollars!"

The class smiles and shakes its head in unison.

FOUR

ROSIE, THE WORLD TRAVELER

Rosie loved to travel. Every Sunday, before macular degeneration robbed her of her sight, she would wash the breakfast dishes and clean up the kitchen and then sit down at the table where she separated the Travel section from the rest of the cumbersome *New York Times* that my father bought at the 7-Eleven half a mile away. With arthritic fingers, she carefully placed the oversized newspaper on the kitchen table and began her trip around the world.

After studying the featured city on the front page, she moved on to the various U.S. destinations: Florida - Miami Beach and Orlando, then on to Maine and New Hampshire, stopping at a few B & Bs in Massachusetts and Connecticut along the way. She luxuriated in hotel suites at The Plaza and St. Moritz Hotels in New York City. A visit to the Mexican Riviera was followed by a Caribbean cruise to San Juan, St. Maartin, and St. Thomas. As the pages unfolded, she ventured out to more exotic destinations, swimming with the turtles in the Galapagos Islands or snorkeling at the Great Barrier Reef in

Australia. Looking for some down time, she took a European river cruise ending at the Tilbury Port in London, returning to JFK Airport on the supersonic Concorde jet.

Turning over the last page of her journey through the "Old Gray Lady's" Travel section, she neatly refolded the paper, removed her glasses and smiled, satisfied that she had just gone around the world!

FIVE

CHEER UP, THINGS COULD BE WORSE

"The only thing worse than being blind is having sight and no vision."

Helen Keller

September, 1990

The room is filled with frustration and despair. An enormous "S L" looms across the wall opposite the nervous patient sitting in a chair. Her legs, too short to reach the floor, are dangling in the darkened room. With some optimism, the doctor points to the second line of the Snellen Eye Chart that he has projected on the screen.

"Can you read this line for me, Mrs. Anderman?" The kindly, white-haired doctor is soft-spoken and patient.

"What line?" she nervously asks.

He moves up to the first line of the chart, displaying a huge single letter "E".

"Just tell me what you see," he gently prods.

"I don't see anything. I guess I'm blind."

I sit on the small bench in the examining room, witnessing this heartbreaking scene. We have come to visit the ophthalmologist because it was becoming more and more difficult for her to see television programs, and she could no longer clearly see the printed words in magazines or newspapers.

This is the second eye specialist my mother has consulted since her vision drastically diminished when suddenly she was unable to see the bright yellow dotted line in the middle of the road. Panic-stricken and without an appointment, she immediately drove herself to her usual eye doctor and entered his office demanding to be seen immediately. She was frightened and emotional, but because the doctor had examined her eyes the previous week, he refused to see her. In fact, he accused her of being drunk and making a scene. Rosie barely ever had even a small alcoholic drink, but the heartless doctor swore that he smelled liquor on her breath. Because of the persistent blisters in her mouth, Rosie regularly used Listerine, and it was the smell of that medication that he noticed. But the unfeeling and uncaring second misogynist from whom my mother sought medical help turned her away when an emergency visit to a retinal specialist might have arrested her bleeding macular degeneration which left her irreversibly blind.

For some reason, I am reminded of a joke my father used to tell:

A man tells his friend for whom things are not going well, "Cheer up, things could be worse." So he cheered up, and things got worse!

SIX

ROSIE, THE SURVIVOR

Through the years, Rosie tried to maintain her equilibrium as new maladies invaded her body by saying out loud to herself, *"Oh, I'm sorry. Surely you have the wrong address! But so many of your buddies have already arrived,"* she said resignedly, *"you may just as well come on in!"* The thoughtful, soft, pleasant voice arising from a smile as sweet as any child's, filled with courage and determination as she said aloud, *"Rosie, Rosie. What am I going to do with you!"* followed by a gentle laugh, evoking in those around her their own smiles and laughter. Suddenly aware that she was placing attention on herself, she would look at me and continue, *"So how are you, Ketzila?"* Free of self-pity, she tolerated her crippled body, maintained her sense of humor, and developed the wisdom that comes from years of suffering combined with an unending and unselfish love for others.

Rosie's longevity surprised everyone, but probably no one more than she, herself. Chronically ill from psoriatic rheumatoid arthritis, thyroid disease, Sjogren's syndrome, congestive heart failure, renal disease, macular degeneration, high blood pressure, chronic obstructive pulmonary disease, and an abdominal aneurysm, she out-lived most of her contemporaries, including all of her sib-lings and childhood friends, all of my father's childhood friends and their spouses, people she had known and loved as an adult, including my children's nanny and long-time friend, Peggy, and her *machitenistas* (mothers of her sons-in-law), some of her nephews, and many friends she had come to know after my father died. When we went to a new doctor and had to check off any diseases from a long list if they applied to my mother, I would joke, "Mom, maybe we should just check off the few dis-eases you *don't* have!" One thing she certainly did not have was any form of dementia. During one conversation, she reminded me that I had already told her something I was now repeating.

"Mom," I said. "It will be very embarrassing to get Alzheimer's before you."

Her mind was sharp, and she never suffered from the terrible incurable sicknesses of envy, chronic com-plaining, or despair.

What can one attribute such longevity for a person so savaged by disease? Her optimism was palpable. At her funeral, all of the eulogies used the metaphor that Ro-sie's cup was always half full - never half empty. She saw only the good in her life and in the people around her. Research has shown that being optimistic reduces the im-pact of stressful situations and increases immune-cell responses. Rosie's equanimity in the wake of stressful medical problems, together with her optimism, certainly added to her longevity.

Rosie was a firm believer in the old adage: *"Want what you have."* Of course, she often wished for a "miracle" to cure her arthritis or to restore her vision, but she was intelligent enough to know that this was not to be. With each mounting ailment, she learned to re-invent the person within her and to adjust to the new bully to invade her body and sap some more of the limited strength it still had. She never let the liabilities that were placed upon her detract from her wonderful assets that she refused to give up. She truly wanted what she had.

Glancing toward the sign on her wall with the old Persian proverb, *"I cried because I had no shoes until I met a man who had no feet,"* she said to me, "Don't forget, *Ketzila,* you may think that others have it better than you, but you never know *vous titzik by yenem* (you never know what's happening with other people). The *lovey-dovey* Hollywood couple will be on the cover of *People* magazine next week announcing their divorce. The *wealthy* man who lives next door is on food stamps. The vivacious woman who looks so healthy is battling Stage 4 lymphoma."

In fact, Rosie often said, "Everyone has their own cross to bear, and if people put their problems in the middle of a room and saw the suffering of others, they would be happy to take their own problems back."

Or could it have been the rituals Rosie faithfully followed over the years that contributed to her longevity? From my earliest recollections, my mother insisted upon taking an afternoon nap. This regimen was given to her by a doctor she had seen during the early stages of her disease. No matter what had to be done or how busy she might be, nothing interfered with her afternoon nap. It was a time when we would all be very quiet because Mommy was resting. When I was a little girl, I would nap with her. I can remember so clearly lying next to her on her bed in the front room on West Sixteenth Street, she on her right side, holding me with her right arm under my head and her left arm draped over my shoulder. I could feel her reassuring constant steady breaths on the back of my neck as she slept, her arms wrapped around me protecting me from the monsters and wild animals I just knew were in the closet waiting to pounce on me.

Perhaps the sixteen aspirins a day she ingested for forty years added to her longevity. Until 1983, when she was hospitalized in the Intensive Care Unit with severe internal bleeding while my father lay in his hospital bed two floors above being treated for his acute leukemia, Rosie took two aspirins, neither coated nor buffered, every three hours, totaling sixteen aspirins a day. When the doctor prohibited her from ever using aspirin again, Rosie smiled and said, "Dr. Sharma. If I died just before my severe bleeding, I could have been written up in the medical journals as being the only person in history who consumed so many aspirins a day for forty years with no harmful side effects!" Could high doses of aspirin have accounted for her longevity? After all, aspirin is touted for preventing stroke and heart attacks. With all of Rosie's ailments, heart attack and stroke were not among them.

With regard to Rosie's relationship with other people, she rarely spoke against anyone. Talking about other people, gossiping, idle talk, negative comments (and even some positive) are described in *Perkei Avos* (*Sayings of Our Fathers*), as *loshon hora*. A person is specifically instructed not to engage in such gossip. Thirty-one Torah commandments relate to *loshon hora,* and entire books are devoted to the importance of avoiding *loshon hora.* It is a concept deeply rooted in the principles of Torah and is not to be taken lightly.

If Rosie didn't like what one of her children did or did not do, she never spoke unkindly about them. She refused to complain that a grandchild didn't call, but instead she reported with great happiness whenever he or she did call. When a neighbor with Alzheimer's kicked my mother in her already swollen painful knee, causing her excruciating pain, instead of yelling at her attacker, my mother actually felt sorry for the demented woman and calmed her apologetic husband, explaining that the "poor soul did not know what she was doing."

If I presented her with a description of behavior that I considered poor judgment or insensitivity on the part of my children, she would not allow herself to engage in *loshon hora*. She mollified my concerns and worries by telling me, *"You can't put an old head on young shoulders!"* Her harshest description of a person's poor behavior was, *"He is complicated."*

She passed no judgment and loved people for who they were, regardless of what they did or did not do. Apparently, not engaging in *loshon hora* dramatically contributes to a person's longevity. It certainly scored a lot of points in the long-life column for Rosie.

PART FOUR

ROSIE, THE HEALER

"Every time you smile at someone, it is an action of love, a gift to that person, a beautiful thing."

Mother Teresa

ONE

SHIMSHEE

"I love those who can smile in trouble, who can gather strength from distress, and grow brave by reflection."

Leonardo DaVinci

"*Shimshee,* are you smiling? *Shimshee, mein leiben* (Simon, my love), I don't *hear* you smiling." The corners of his lips slowly form a smile while he is lying very still in his hospital bed with chemicals dripping into his veins in an effort to put him into remission from his acute leukemia. He is fighting for his life; but despite his severe physical discomfort and total exhaustion, if Rosie wanted him to smile, by golly, he would smile!

Shimshee was her pet name for my father. He was the love of her life who stole her heart all those years ago on a lake surrounded by mountains in upstate New York. He owned a cleaning store in Greenwich Village, and his mundane job consisted of cleaning other people's clothes and making alterations on their ill-fitting outfits. He was such a skilled tailor that wealthy customers trusted him to alter their expensive designer clothes. Growing up, surrounded by three accomplished seamstresses (his mother worked in a sweat shop and his two sisters were fashion designers) and without a father figure in the home, it was no wonder that he had become interested in sewing. One of his favorite jokes was: "I can't understand it. I shortened the pants twice and they're still too short!"

Besides the work he did in his cleaning store, he longed to express his creative inner self. He was an avid reader and a prolific writer of short stories that were written with fluidity and filled with great imagery. He purchased oil paints and brushes, an easel, and a pallet and perused magazines for interesting pictures to paint. Some, like the New York City skyline, were advertisements; others were small thumbprints of paintings of the masters that caught his eye. At night, after a day's work of sorting, spotting, cleaning, pressing, and hanging up clothes, he set up his easel and oil paints and taught himself how to copy the pictures he had meticulously cut out from magazines. He was not intimidated by the fame of those painters whose masterpieces he copied. Painstakingly, he prepared a grid of small boxes and then proceeded to copy the picture section by section. Rather than making an exact duplicate of the original painting, he often modified the originals. They were not mere photograph-like exact replicas. The eyes he painted of *The Girl With the Pearl Earring* by Johannes Vermeer were brighter and more alive, and the corners of her mouth were turned up into a more genuine smile. Putting his own personality into his interpretations of the paintings, he made the eyes brighter, the smiles happier, the skies bluer, and the colors more robust.

He loved to read and never failed to have a dictionary handy while reading in case he stumbled across a word he did not recognize. To me, his vocabulary seemed limitless. When I had to define words for English class, I consulted my father rather than the dictionary. My teachers always complimented me on how concise, precise, and accurate my definitions were!

Even though he put in long and grueling hours working in his dry cleaning store, he found the time to take violin lessons, and he studied with the same virtuoso who taught my brother and me to play. He was probably not only the oldest but also the most serious student of Mr. Ricco at the Greenwich House Music School. On the evenings when he didn't set up his easel to paint, he would unfold his music stand and practice the violin long into the night.

Decades before it was in vogue, my father was extremely health conscious. He read the labels on cans of food, exercised every morning, and led us in healthy family rituals. When we lived on Sixteenth Street just outside Greenwich Village in New York City, he had us sit around the metal-top kitchen table so popular in the 1940s, the table with the built-in cutlery drawer and the carved oak base. It was my job to dust the ornate pedestal because I was the smallest with the littlest hands to reach into all of the crevices. The table was against the wall under the window that opened onto the fire escape. The other wall had the dumbwaiter, a pulley-like elevator where we put our garbage to send down to the cellar where Mr. Moss, the superintendent of the brownstone building, removed it and, as if by magic, returned the empty garbage can back to the kitchen.

Sitting at the table, my father carefully measured out a teaspoonful of cod liver oil and served it to each of us (my mother, my sister, my brother, me, and to himself) in order to ward off disease. Then came the eye exercises. Watching my father intently as he led the routine, we followed him in unison as we looked up, looked down, rolled our eyes around clockwise, then counterclockwise, then diagonally from upper right to lower left and vice-versa. (Fifty years later, sitting on the floor of the basement of my yoga instructor in Teaneck, New Jersey, I was brought back in time when, unexpectedly, the teacher duplicated the exact eye exercises my father had taken us through on Sixteenth Street!)

When we moved to the old rooming house in Spring Valley, he taught himself how to renovate the decaying structure. He installed new plumbing, replaced frayed electrical wiring, bought a cement mixer and poured concrete, and painted the entire place inside and out. He even figured out how to build a swimming pool.

On his own, he became a plumber, an electrician, a mason, a painter of houses and of art, a musician, a writer, and an all-around handyman.

Above all, he was a devoted husband to a chronically ailing wife and a loving father, who taught us all how to drive a car, hang a picture, paint a room, and gave us insight into human nature. His energy level kept up with his aspirations, and he looked forward to accomplishing so many more things until acute leukemia stopped him in his tracks, leaving him immobile in the ICU being asked to smile by Rosie. His will and her willfulness pulled him through this time, but after a one-year remission, as the fatalistic line in the song "Found a Peanut" tells us, he "died anyway" on September 21, 1984. He probably said to himself,

"I can't understand it. I went through chemotherapy for my leukemia twice, and I still died from leukemia!"

TWO

STEVEN

"Grandma. Tomorrow I'm going to watch the sunrise at the Grand Canyon!" It was Steven calling from California, telling Rosie of his exciting plans for the following day.

After her *Shimshee* died, my mother started to get her affairs in order, and it looked as though she wanted to throw in the towel. She kept her daily routine but was sad and lonely most of the time. Eight months later, her first grandchild died at the age of twenty-three. She had lost the love of her life and the apple of her eye in one fell swoop. The pain was agonizing. But instead of wallowing in her losses, she rallied, found renewed strength, and resumed her matriarchal position in the family.

January 27, 1995

On the occasion of what would have been Steven's thirty-third birthday, I went to the library and read a short story by Gabriel Garcia Marquez. Ten years earlier, just before Steven's tragic fatal accident, he had recommended that I read *One Hundred Years of Solitude* also by Gabriel Garcia Marquez. I never read it. But on this day, I wanted to do something that connected me to my wonderful nephew. I found myself walking into the library, perusing the "New Books" section, finding *Strange Pilgrims* by Gabriel Garcia Marquez, sitting down in the library's reading area, and reading the prologue and the first of the twelve short stories contained in the book.

In his prologue, Marquez describes a dream in which he is attending his own funeral, "walking with a group of friends dressed in solemn mourning but in a festive mood." It was only when all of his friends started to leave that the dreamer realized that he could not leave with them; and "only then did [he] understand that dying means never being with friends again."

Gabriel Garcia Marquez is lucky. It was only a dream; and even though Steven was also a dreamer, his death was no dream at all. It was harsh, unfair, inexplicable, and sudden. It was unbearably real.

Yes, Steven was definitely a dreamer. Which of his dreams would have been realized? Which dreams would have come true?

Would he have married the girl of his dreams he told Rosie about? The girl he loved and who, tragically, I met for the first time at Steven's funeral.

Would he have published stories or perhaps written songs for guitar or piano that would become familiar tunes in everyone's household?

Would his name have appeared as the director or producer in the credits of a movie that he dreamt about writing? Would he have lived in Hollywood, where he had been visiting just before he embarked on his fateful, fatal trip to return to New Jersey by car?

Would he have become an international traveler, practicing his French in Paris or learning Spanish in Madrid?

Would he have demonstrated the artistic skills that he got from his grandfather and become a painter of modern art or pastural scenes?

Perhaps he would have followed a path of university teaching - Philosophy or English Literature, his major studies at Princeton.

Maybe he would just have enjoyed a nine-to-five job, supporting a loving family with children who adored him as I did.

But his final dream was to watch the sunrise at the Grand Canyon with all of his other dreams barely imagined. Driving through the night from Los Angeles, he fell asleep at the wheel and his car struck a tree, killing him instantly as he exited the highway at Flagstaff, just seventy-five miles from his destination. Steven never did get to see the sunrise at the Grand Canyon. It was a cruel turn of events that changed his enthusiastic anticipation of the sunrise into the final sunset of his life. It was an instant in his life that changed his dreams into the worst nightmare imaginable.

THREE

CHANALA

"*Chanala*, what made you sick?" At the young age of twelve, my mother tried to comfort her two-year-old baby sister, Chana, who was dying from complications of the measles. It was an epidemic that took the lives of several toddlers in their Brooklyn apartment building. John Enders would not develop the measles vaccine for another forty years. Rosie (who was called by her Yiddish name *Raisl*) shared a room with Chana. When the baby was very sick, people asked her, "Who made you so sick?" Her reply was "Ai-u (*Raisl*) make me sick." Then, when she was on death's doorstep, she said, "Ai-u no make me sick. Me make me sick."

Rosie tried to comfort the dying child, singing to her and playing games with her: *Peek-a-Boo* and *This Little Piggy*. She came home from school and tried to amuse the sick child by reciting the poem by Robert Louis Stevenson she had just memorized called *My Shadow*:

> *"I have a little shadow that goes in and out*
> *with me,*
> *And what can be the use of him is more than*
> *I can see.*

> *He is very, very like me from the heels up to*
> *the head;*
> *And I see him jump before me, when I jump*
> *into my bed."*

She probably used the same sing-song soothing voice she would use twenty years later when I couldn't fall asleep because of nightmares. At night, she sang the Yiddish lullaby, *"Oifn Pripetshik"* ("At the Hearth") - in her comforting, slightly off-key voice as she stroked her brow to soothe the baby to sleep.

> *"In the little hearth flickers a little flame,*
> *Warmth spreads through the house,*
> *And the rabbi teaches little children*
> *The Hebrew Aleph-bet (alphabet)."*

Sometimes she sang the old Welsh lullaby:

> *"Sleep my child, and peace attend thee,*
> *all through the night.*
> *Guardian angels God will lend thee,*
> *all through the night."*

As a mother, years later, she would sing the same lullabies to coax me into slumber.

* * * * *

But no one could prevent the impending doom, and all Rosie could do was to try to abate the child's fear and pain. She recalled this heart-wrenching memory when she told it to me some seventy years later, and the tears in her eyes and quivering in her voice reflected the pain she still felt after so many decades.

* * * * *

Well-meaning neighbors tried to console my grandmother by reminding her that she had six other children, to which she replied, "If someone cuts off one of your ten fingers, does it bleed any less because you have nine left?"

So distraught over the death of Chana, she decided to have another child.

And thus Uncle Manny was born.

FOUR

UNCLE MANNY

"Manny, now that Mama is gone, you'll live with us and be a part of our family," Rosie tells her baby brother.

When my Uncle Manny was so devastated by the death of his mother that he didn't know where to turn, it was Rosie who unselfishly invited him to live with us. Her reassuring words were just what he needed to hear. At the age of six, I could not fathom his strong emotional reaction to the loss of his mother. If I only knew! I certainly do now.

The five years he lived with us until we moved to Spring Valley in 1955 were filled with fun and excitement. He was always taking us places and buying us things. Money was no object when it came to entertaining us and enjoying himself, and he always made sure he had plenty of time to spend with us.

He took us to the Penny Arcades on 42nd Street in New York City, where we played Skee-ball, when Times Square was a child's wonderland before peep shows and X-rated movies invaded the neighborhood. He entertained me with castanets when I broke my arm soon after one of his many weekend trips to Cuba where the exciting nightlife, casinos and clubs attracted wealthy Americans before Castro came into power. He took us to the movies, taught us how to play blackjack and poker, and took us for drives in his 1954 white Thunderbird convertible sports car. One day, he brought home five Schwinn bicycles: one for each of my siblings, one for each of my twin cousins and, of course, one for me. Mine was dark green with fat wheels. How I loved that bike! He bought me a big gray life-sized stuffed poodle that he saw in a shop window because it had a sign that said that it was the *Doggie in the Window* Rosemary Clooney referred to in her hit song by the same name. Later, he brought home a real puppy and showered us with ice cream, candy, and toys. Uncle Manny was the quintessential bachelor uncle. He was the uncle of every child's dreams. He and I had a very special relationship, even though he often teased me, saying, "You were so ugly when you were born that I enlisted in the army three days later on my eighteenth birthday!"

For a number of years, Uncle Manny lived on top of the world. A partner in his brothers' foam rubber business (the feather business had recovered from the Great Depression and had evolved into a successful foam rubber establishment), Uncle Manny was a very wealthy man. He traveled, spending weekends in Cuba, Miami Beach, and Las Vegas (or "Lost Wages" as he referred to

59

"Sin City"). He had a magnificent apartment in Sheepshead Bay in Brooklyn, overlooking Long Island Sound, where he had one bedroom filled with several large fish tanks to breed his guppies. There was nothing else in that room but fish! He shopped at the upscale men's store, Barney's, which was located around the corner from us on Sixteenth Street, and he bought expensive furniture for my parents' newly acquired, but very old and run-down rooming house. Uncle Manny indulged us in anything and everything we ever could want.

But then his life fell apart. From living the *Life of Riley* - fancy clothes, a beautiful apartment, and exotic vacations - he hit rock bottom. Because he squandered all of his money on an extravagant lifestyle, his finances plummeted. He began to drink excessively, and he ended up attached to a respirator in the Intensive Care Unit at Kings County Hospital after he was found unconscious in his dingy, filthy, dilapidated one-room furnished apartment in Brighton Beach. When I visited him in the ICU, he looked so frightened, unable to talk yet conscious enough to experience the pain of the respirator tube, staring at the clock. After he was taken off the respirator, he told me that he watched the second hand of the clock move around and around, ticking off each second until he was freed from the terrible ordeal. From there, he was transferred to the Veterans Administration Hospital on Twenty-Third Street in Manhattan, where he was diagnosed with a blood clot in the brain and poor circulation.

He was sick enough to be transferred to the V. A. Hospital in Bath, New York, where he died a dozen years later, two days before Labor Day. That was when he went to the infirmary because he was having shortness of breath and chest pain. Four hours later, he died of a heart attack. I spoke to the nurse who was on duty that night. She told me that his heart went into ventricular fibrillation (rapid erratic heartbeats); and unable to keep from crying, she told me that he died in her arms. I was happy that when he took his final breath, he was with someone he knew and who obviously cared for him.

He had named me his next of kin, and I was sent all of his personal belongings: four pairs of polyester pants, two pairs of worn out vinyl shoes, three pairs of eyeglasses, two sets of false teeth, a portable radio, two Timex watches (one working and one broken), a few misshapen plastic belts with varying worn-out holes indicating his weight losses, five stained shirts, and a pair of pajamas. These were the final possessions of a man who had owned a limited edition 1954 Thunderbird convertible, had outfitted himself at Barney's, and who had bought only the best and most expensive designer clothes and shoes.

FIVE

AUNT SOPHIE

"Rose. Rose. What am I going to do?"

I was only three years old, but I still recall the agony of my Aunt Sophie as she walked around in circles in the living room of her apartment on East Second Street in Brooklyn. Just a few hours earlier, at one in the morning, a policeman rapped on the door of her second-floor apartment. My twelve-year-old cousin, Fay, trudged to the door.

"Does Mrs. Meister live here?" he asked.

"Yes," replied the girl, still half asleep.

"Tell her that Abraham Meister died of a heart attack at work."

No one expected a forty-eight-year-old strapping, healthy man to drop dead at the knitting factory where he was the night manager. Aunt Sophie had met him at the Henry Street Settlement House on the Lower East Side of New York. She was immediately smitten by him, but she was only fourteen and could not act on her feelings toward a man five years her senior. He was only too happy to follow his adventurous instincts and traveled on freight trains to explore the country. Ten years later, she saw him again, this time old enough to snag his attention, and they were married in 1930. He liked to paint, but his greatest love was singing. He and Jan Peerce both auditioned at the Metropolitan Opera House, and even though Uncle Abie's voice was as exceptional as the famous tenor's, it was Jan Peerce who got the job (reportedly because Uncle Abie wore Coke-bottle thick eyeglasses and did not look like a professional singer).

Who could have known that his untimely death would have caused the early demise of my Aunt Sophie. Everything in life has a consequence, even death. After Uncle Abie died, Aunt Sophie left her job as a dressmaker in a local Brooklyn boutique and went to work as a tailor in my father's dry cleaning store where she sat behind her old and worn Singer sewing machine in the window of my father's store on the corner of Fourteenth Street and Seventh Avenue in New York City.

Every day after school, I would go to the grocery store two doors away to buy her a Dannon yogurt (decades before yogurt became the "in" thing to eat), an orange, and a box of Uneeda Biscuits. She ate healthy foods long before it was in vogue, but her diet could not ward off the deadly effects of the chemicals that eventually killed her.

Five years before my father succumbed to the poisonous fumes of carbon tetrachloride and perchloroethylene (which we knew as "carbon tet" and "perc"), the same insidious killer, leukemia, claimed the life of my jovial Aunt Sophie.

Sandwiched between her two surviving siblings (my older more staid and intellectual Aunt Sarah and her baby brother, who was my quiet and kind practical father), Aunt Sophie did not even try to compete with either sibling on any level. She had her own unique personality, fun-loving and joyful even in the wake of sorrow. Widowed at a young age with two small daughters, she was always cheerful and fun to be around. She used wonderful words of endearment, like *Toots* and *Honey*, and I always felt loved whenever I was around her. She put my hair in pin-curls and took me to Lindy's for ice cream and Nathan's for hot dogs. We saw the *Holiday Show* at Radio City and went to the movies to see *Marjorie Morningstar* and *Somebody Up There Likes Me*.

A visit to Aunt Sophie's apartment was always a treat. I slept in her room and was awakened by the sun streaming through the venetian blinds early in the morning. It was there that she prepared holiday meals, snapping the ends off of string beans while she stood by the sink with a dish towel flung over her shoulder.

Everybody should have an Aunt Sophie!

SIX

UNCLE HYMIE

"Hymie. We're the *outlaws!*" Rosie and Uncle Hymie were the only two in-laws. Almost everyone in the family found Uncle Hymie disagreeable and merely tolerated him. His wife (my father's sister, Sarah), Rosie, and I truly loved him.

It was October, 1988. With a twinkle in his eyes and a smile upon his lips, at the age of ninety-seven, on his deathbed at Coney Island Hospital with one leg amputated, lying in his own excrement, blind, weighing barely more than the sum total of his skeleton, he states *"If I knew I was going to live this long, I would have taken better care of myself!"* He inquires about Nicaragua and the Iran-Contra Affair and the upcoming presidential race between Vice President George H. W. Bush and the governor of Massachusetts, Michael Dukakis. Looking at his gangrenous remaining leg, he objectively asks, without emotion, about a new plastic that can be used in healing open wounds. He asks me to try to find out where to buy an electronic device he has read about, one that emits a certain frequency of sound that can repel the mice inhabiting his little bungalow in Brighton Beach.

Hyman S. Berger held a degree in pharmacy from the Brooklyn College of Pharmacy dated May 11, 1918, and he never stopped learning. He could hold a brilliant conversation about chemical engineering, politics, or history.

He and his missus (he always referred to Aunt Sarah as his "missus") owned a drugstore on the corner of Willoughby and Marcy Avenues in Brooklyn. There, I would play with the pay phone made of solid oak where you held the elongated earpiece that was connected to a long cord attached to the side of the phone to your ear and leaned in to speak into the mouthpiece that was built into the front of the phone. I used to look at the dozen books in the small lending library that he loaned out to customers for a few cents a week, and I watched in awe as he crushed medications with a wooden mortar and pestle and carefully poured them into gelatinous capsules, thus filling prescriptions for specialized compounds. Was it any wonder, then, that decades later, he was revered by his Brighton Beach neighbors who never filled a prescription before consulting with him.

"*Mista Boiga* (Mr. Berger). Is it okay for me to take this medicine?"

After he sold his drug store, he and his missus move to a dilapidated two-bedroom shack eight blocks from the Brighton Beach boardwalk. One bedroom was filled with a collection of discards he found on the street. There was an assortment of broken furniture, old books, a vintage dress form, a malfunctioning sewing machine, and an array of other junk strewn all over the room in a rather precarious way. He never drove a car and walked everywhere, picking up other people's castoffs, including an outdated set of encyclopedias, which he read from cover to cover.

To me, he was the grandfather I never had. He had a kind, gentle face with soft gray eyes that crinkled at the corners when he smiled. His flat nose was a result of a surgery he underwent for free while in the army to correct a breathing disorder. It did not work. His breathing got worse and his nose lost its cartilage and collapsed onto his face. But it didn't cost him anything so he figured he got his money's worth! He retold this story over and over again as matter-of-factly as if he were telling me that bread cost three cents back then and the trolley was a nickel.

More than half a century earlier, he suffered from gastroenteritis. He consulted a doctor of homeopathic medicine who prescribed a special diet for him which included cooked bananas, hot water and honey, and a day of fasting once a week. It cured him. But his strict diet didn't prevent him from munching on his famous sesame candies that he always had on hand and doled out liberally to all the children in the family when they came to visit.

He was an avid walker, a source of wonderful stories, and an ever-flowing fountain of knowledge. A medic in World War I, The Great War, the war that was to end

all wars, he had been born on August 21, 1891, some-
where in Austria. I used to listen in awe when he told me
how his father had abandoned him when he was a baby
and later kidnapped him when he was a young boy. He
never said this sadly nor with any bitterness, rather always
with an amused smile on his lips and a twinkle in his eye.
When he relayed any adversity that he had encountered
in his almost century of life, he was philosophical and hu-
morous, never trite or morbid.

Orphaned as a teenager, he had lived in France
and moved to America to live with relatives. Unhappy
though his childhood seemed and having been shuttled
from relative to relative, he would lovingly spar with my
Aunt Sarah, *"Why did I ever leave my happy home for
you?"* Childless, he was jealous of the love that his wife
heaped on her mother and nieces. It is said that he once
tried to forcibly "usher" my grandmother out of his house.
He didn't want any competition with the attention of his
missus.

My cousins and my siblings didn't have the patience to listen to his long-winded stories. Because I was
the only one who loved to walk with him, using two, three,
or maybe even four of my baby steps to each of his long
strides, and because I was always in awe of all of his stories, I knew I was his favorite. I never grew tired of the
long walks nor of the true stories about his life that rivaled
any fiction I had ever read.

His missus joined him four-and-a-half years later on April 18, 1992. Together, they witnessed the First World War; marveled at the first airplane flight; lived through the amazing transition of transportation from horse and buggy to the motor car; saw the invention of the washing machine (revolutionizing the role of women in the workplace by liberating them from the time-consuming chore of washing clothes by hand) (1907), the radio (1913), the refrigerator (1922), "talkies" (when the darlings of silent films like Rudolph Valentino and Mary Pickford exposed their voices and failed to make the transition in 1922), television (1925), and antibiotics (which, if invented ten years earlier in 1915, might have saved Aunt Sarah's two siblings, Joseph and Rose). Even the Band-Aid didn't make it into their drug store until 1920!

SEVEN

AUNT SARAH

"Sarah. Do you want a cigarette?"

Rosie used to tell me that Aunt Sarah liked to smoke *yenems.*

"What brand of cigarettes are those?" I asked.

"You know. Other people's cigarettes," she laughed.

My father's oldest sister Sarah and Rosie had an ongoing love-hate relationship. Were the rumors true that she wanted my mother to have an abortion when she was pregnant with my sister or that she told my father to leave my mother after Rosie invited some of her girlfriends to what Aunt Sarah considered an extravagant luncheon that she could ill-afford? But this did not seem to detract from the deep-seated love they had for each other. After all, they both unconditionally loved the same man - my father!

Ever since I can remember, Aunt Sarah was a short plump woman with wispy gray hair, a multi-linguist who loved learning and absolutely adored her baby brother, my father, who was thirteen years her junior. She used to bring me tiny packages of Chiclets chewing gum that she bought in subway vending machines for a penny and traveled all the way from Brooklyn to Manhattan to bring me cough medicine from her drugstore when I was sick. When I was pregnant with my first child, she drew a pattern on brown paper and taught me how to sew my first maternity dress made out of the fabric used for the curtains that we salvaged from the dressing room of my father's cleaning store. Aunt Sarah was a great source of knowledge and gave me practical advice. One such pearl of wisdom that I often find useful in my life is, *"If you try to please everyone, you end up pleasing no one, especially not yourself!"*

In 1991, when she was ninety-five years old, a group of Anderman descendants organized a trip to her birthplace, Buchach, a small town that had been located in Austria when she and my father lived there. (Subsequently it was taken over by Poland in 1918 and is now part of Ukraine). I asked Aunt Sarah if she was going.

Her reply was, "No, I'm too old."

I asked her if she wasn't too old would she go.

She answered, "Carol, before World War II, about 10,000 Jews lived in Buchach. By 1944, the year you were born, only about 100 Jewish survivors remained. So in answer to your question about visiting Buchach - *Absolutely not.* They hated the Jews *then.* They hate the Jews *now.* So why would I go!"

Of course, escaping persecution in Europe was a major reason for coming to America, but it was not the precipitating factor.

Seven months before she died, I took her to the boardwalk on her beloved Brighton Beach in Coney Island for the last time. That was when I learned how and why she came to America. I had always imagined that she came to America alone at the age of sixteen to escape persecution as a Jew in Buchach. I imagined her leaving behind her widowed mother and four siblings to find a better life for them and for herself in America. Indeed, Aunt Sarah had come to America when she was sixteen, and she left behind her mother and siblings, of whom my father was the youngest. But she came to America not only to find wealth and to escape anti-semitism but to fulfill a secret personal passion.

Her family, who traded livestock and sold cattle to the Czar, was prominent in Buchach. But my aunt loved beautiful clothes and dreamed of becoming a dress designer. As she explained to me, eight decades after making the journey to America, becoming a seamstress was out of the question because it was beneath her social class and doing so would embarrass her family. So, unbeknownst to her mother, Aunt Sarah wrote to an aunt who lived in New York and asked her to send a ticket for passage to America. Her aunt sent the ticket, and on May 20, 1912, at the age of sixteen, Aunt Sarah made her way to Rotterdam, Holland, and as Passenger #103623050170, she boarded the SS Rotterdam bound for America. Here, she worked as a dressmaker, making and designing clothes. She fashioned clothing patterns for women whose figures were similar to hers who did not fit into the regular sizes, and she created what was to become "half sizes." She made a handsome living and sent for her mother and her siblings the following year.

She often reminisced about her early life, which was filled with both love and heartache. Before she emigrated to America, her father, Alexander Zishsa, a Torah scholar, died at the age of forty-one of kidney failure. Two baby brothers also died in Europe. One brother fell while ice-skating, and the broken bone perforated his leg, leading to infection and eventual death. The other baby died after he hit his head on the ceiling while an older relative was throwing him in the air in fun-loving playfulness. Another brother, Joseph, died in New York of a mastoid ear infection when he was a teenager; and her "beautiful little sister Rose" bled to death from ulcerative colitis when she was twelve. My grandmother lost her husband and four children before she reached the age of forty. No wonder the photographs I have of her when she was in her forties look like a woman in her eighties. My father, the baby, only three years old when he arrived in America and Aunt Sophie, five years older, became the focal points of my aunt's love and devotion.

At her funeral, the rabbi said, "When an old person dies, it is like a library burning down."

Why hadn't I perused the card catalogue or at least browsed through the fiction and nonfiction, biography and autobiography sections? Why had I merely waltzed through the splendor of the aging edifice foolishly expecting it to be there forever for me to explore at my leisure?

EIGHT

ME

"Don't worry, *Ketzila*. Give her some Milk of Magnesia or some Maalox. You'll see, she'll be fine."

I tried to hide my fear and frustration as I impatiently told my mother, "Emily's condition is far worse than anything that the old die-hard remedy of your generation can cure."

My sweet and gentle nine-year-old Emily had been suffering from what initially seemed like an unrelenting stomach virus. It had been going on for over a week, and she could not stop vomiting. Living in a medical environment is not always a good thing. After looking through my husband's medical textbooks, I came to the awful, absolutely erroneous, conclusion that Emily's strange symptoms were the result of a brain tumor! So concerned about her condition, I spoke by telephone with a pediatric gastroenterologist who worked at Mount Sinai Hospital in New York and after describing the symptoms to him in great detail, he told me that although the virus that had caused the symptoms in the first place had probably disappeared, the esophagus had become so irritated from the intense vomiting that the urge to vomit persisted.

What was the remedy for Emily's symptoms by this world-renowned pediatric gastroenterologist? Maalox. Three times a day for three months! I thanked him and when I told him that was what my mother had suggested, I could see his smile even over the telephone. With great admiration for my mother's expertise not only on child-rearing but on medical advice as well, I related to her what the doctor had recommended. She joked that given all her ailments, she was an "A.A.D." (Almost A Doctor); but she never said, "I told you so."

PART FIVE

SIGNS

ONE

December 22, 2000

Judaism teaches that God sends signs to us, perhaps to guide us or to prepare us for events that would otherwise be impossible to bear or maybe to humble us when our egos grow too large. There are no such phenomena as coincidences. Things happen for a reason.

Every *Shabbos* (the Sabbath), I light candles for each of my children, for my husband and myself, and one for my mother who has been chronically ill for many years. The candles always burn brightly and fully until the wax or oil, depending on the type of medium I use, has been completely consumed and the glass candle holder is depleted of all sources of energy. I keep my candlesticks on the same table and in the same position, to which, after cleaning, I carefully return them each week.

The last three Friday nights, when I have covered my eyes and said my prayers after lighting the candles, there is one candle, always the one I have allocated to my mother, that flickers for a short time; and while all the others continue to burn for several hours, this one struggles for a few minutes and then, for no apparent reason, goes out. The first time this happens, I think perhaps some outside physical force has extinguished it. Could there be an undetectable breeze or maybe the candlestick is bent in some way? Perhaps the wick on that particular candle is not straight or too short or has gotten wet somehow.

After the second time the candle spontaneously and prematurely self-extinguishes, I begin to wonder if, in fact, this is a sign to prepare me for my mother's death. I envision the struggling flame as a metaphor of my mother's fate. Her health has been steadily declining. Breathing is more difficult; infections are more frequent; she has been less talkative and is becoming more forgetful.

When the candle goes out for the third time, I cannot resist rekindling it, even though it is forbidden to do so on *Shabbos* according to Jewish law. Once a *Shabbos* candle goes out, it is not permissible to relight it. Once again, I search for a reason for its obstinacy. Could there be a draft, poor positioning, or a defective wick? Even after correcting all of the possible outside physical causes, within a matter of moments, the flame flickers and dies.

There is no question in my mind that this is truly a sign, a warning, a foreboding, an omen to prepare me for the inevitable. So when Emma, Rosie's home health aide, calls in a panic to tell me that she has had to use mouth-to-mouth resuscitation to revive my mother after her body had become limp and her speech incoherent, I am frightened and saddened, but not surprised.

January 6, 2001

Two weeks later, after lighting the *Shabbos* candle I have designated for my mother, I am relieved that it does not go out. But shortly thereafter, my relief turns to despair when the glass holder of the very same candlestick cracks and breaks. Another sign? Does the inner flame still burn brightly when the outer body becomes feeble and shatters?

When we think of loved ones who are very ill or no longer with us, do we recall them in their weak and deteriorated state, or do we see them as they were in the height of their glory?

Their essence - that inner flame - is what remains eternal. Their love, lessons, and loyalty constitute their legacies, not the crumbling bodies that succumb to illness and disease.

TWO

January 26, 2001

Signs. Signs. They are all over the place, sometimes subtle, sometimes painfully clear. January 26, 2001,
three days before my mother is to take her final breath, I
am with her in the emergency room at Valley Hospital.
We have been together all night. She has severe pain in
her hip and in her abdomen, and they are trying to deter-
mine its source. Could she have dislocated her artificial
hip? Is she experiencing some sort of heart problem? The
diagnosis is not clear. They are sending her home.

The patient in the next cubicle has been transferred from the emergency room to a regular hospital
room. The cubicle is empty. And then I notice it - the
sign. My eyes fall upon it, and it is too late. I have seen
it and there is nothing I can do. It is just laying there,
seemingly innocuous and unthreatening. But as a sign, it
is clear and frightening. The wrapper, transparent, sterile,
official, medical, is clearly labeled "Post-Mortem Mask".
I avert my eyes, but not soon enough. I have already seen
it. The damage is done. The sign is clear. The message
is delivered. It cannot be undone.

PART SIX

SUPERSTITIONS

ONE

JUST IN CASE!

After my father's funeral, we were all sitting outside. Someone sneezed, and Rosie insisted that he pull his left ear. He smiled his sweet smile at his Grandma - the one who had known her the longest among all the grandchildren. But he wouldn't pull his ear. Such a foolish thing to do, he thought.

It was a silly superstition, a *bubbe meise*, an old wives' tale that we had all grown up with. If you sneezed while talking about the dead, you were supposed to pull your left ear so the same fate would not befall you. But he didn't. He didn't humor his Grandma even though it was just a superstition or maybe because that was all it was. Seven-and-a-half months later, he was dead.

When he was a little boy, he wanted to know what happened to you after you died. His Grandma told him that you go to Heaven.

"No, you don't," he said matter-of-factly. "You get buried in the ground."

* * * * *

I dreamed that my father was sitting at a table in Heaven. When he looked up, he asked in a startled tone, "Steven, what are you doing here!"

"I guess I should've listened to Grandma," he answered with a twinkle in his eye.

* * * * *

Rosie's superstitions are silly, I guess. But if we are talking about someone who is dead or if I am thinking about a deceased person and if I should sneeze during the course of this conversation or thought, my left hand automatically reaches for my ear. I don't actually pull it, but I allow my fingers to brush along the lobe ever so lightly so that what I am doing doesn't seem so conspicuous. But there is no question that I am fully aware of the significance of this ritual.

TWO

ALL THAT GLITTERS IS NOT GOLD

It glitters in the sunlight, laying on the ground, small but powerful, beautiful but dangerous, taunting me, baiting me to pick it up. "Come on, sucker, pick me up."

"Forget it!" I mumble to myself. A stranger might think I was hallucinating, but I don't care. I won't ever fall for that again, not ever.

"Find a penny and pick it up, and all day long you'll have good luck."

I was walking with Rosie, reveling in a beautiful day in May. The sun was shining and the glint of the new penny twinkling on the sidewalk was irresistible, so I leaned over to pick it up.

"Don't pick it up, *Ketzila,*" admonished my mother. "It won't bring you luck."

"Nonsense!" I replied. So I scooped it up, admiring not only its beauty but also what it stood for.

It was May 7, 1985. I was happy. The fine weather was intoxicating. Spring was in the air. What better way to add to my sense of well-being than to snap up the seductive penny to complete the joy I was feeling. Twenty-four hours later, we got the dreaded phone call. We were notified that my nephew, Steven, was killed in a car accident in Arizona - the shiny penny most likely spent and gone, like my bright and shining nephew speeding to the Grand Canyon to catch the sunrise.

How many times since then have I been tempted by the enticing metallic glint winking at me from under a car or behind a pole, seeing it out of the corner of my eye. Sometimes, it is bold and brazen, exposing itself on a walkway or on the carpet of a hallway, in plain view right in front of me. Imagine the audacity to lure me like that as if there was no history to its potentially diabolic powers. How dare you! Who do you think you are! How stupid do you think I am!

PART SEVEN

LIFE WITHOUT ROSIE

ONE

BETWEEN TWO WORLDS
January 28, 2001

The Intensive Care Unit. The end is near. The aneurysm is slowly dissecting, ripping the sensitive wall of the aorta, causing excruciating pain. There is kidney failure and precipitously falling blood pressure. The mother who used to soothe and comfort me with her steady, even breaths when I was a little girl now looks as though she has been barely saved from a drowning accident. Gasping and struggling, her chest heaving in and out, her concentration is solely on getting in the next breath of air. Irregular breathing and terrible pain are controlled by morphine – as much as she needs. She is not comatose but in a deep sleep. I rub her forehead for hours, singing to her the songs she sang to me: *The Anniversary Waltz*, *"Oh, how we danced on the night we were wed . . . ."* She loved that song - her wedding song. I hum Yiddish songs she used to sing. I try to remember the tunes. We were listening to them together a mere three weeks before. I sing a medley: *"When you walk through a storm, hold your head up high and don't be afraid of the dark,"* *"You are my sunshine, my only sunshine. You make me happy when skies are gray."* My voice cracks as tears well up in my eyes, but I continue. I am on autopilot, not thinking about the songs. They just pour out from my heart. I try to sing *A Yiddishe Momma (A Jewish Mother)*, one of the Yiddish songs my mother loved to sing; but I only know the first three words and the tune. Then, my father's old favorites that my parents sang while driving from Spring Valley to New York City, we three children in the backseat trying to follow the tunes of *My Blue Heaven - "I see a quiet place, a fireplace, a honeymoon. A little nest to nestle where the roses bloom. Just Rosie and me. And baby makes three. Together in my blue heaven." "Found a Peanut, Found a Peanut, Found a Peanut Last Night." "My Wife She Comes from Cincinnati, and there she was so happy and fatty."* Tit Willow - *"On a tree by the river sat little Tom Tit, Tit Willow, Tit Willow, Tit Willow"* (why was Daddy saying "tit"?) *"Oh, Where Do You Work A-John. On the Delaware Lackawan. And what do you do a-John? Oh, I push, I push, I push."* I hear myself singing *Where is Love?*, *On My Own*, and *Bei Mir Bistu Shein (To Me You Are Beautiful)* - all the while stroking her forehead and choking up. In between, I flood her with words of love and kisses. She is peaceful. Her breathing is steady and relaxed. I tell her how all of her children, grandchildren, and great-grandchildren love her. I say each of their names. She knows what I am saying.

Suddenly, there is pain. She grimaces, moans, and becomes agitated. Steve never leaves her side.

"Is he her son?" asks the nurse.

She is surprised that a son-in-law would be so attentive, so concerned, so loving. Steve, the physician, asks the nurse to give his mother-in-law more morphine. The effect is almost immediate. I continue rubbing her head. I sing, and when tears well up and I am too choked up to sing the words, I hum. Steve holds my hand and squeezes it. He hums along, too, as he holds my mother's small deformed hand, now bruised from all the IVs. He adjusts the IV. It is obviously bothering her but not like the back pain from the aneurysm that will kill her. I feel weak. My knees feel like rubber. I step back - away from her for a moment. "Stay with her. She needs you." I know that what Steve says is true. I would say that to myself. My strength is regained as I hold her hand and stroke her brow. I tell her how she would do this to me when I was a little girl afraid to go to sleep. Shadows from the curtains formed animal shapes on the ceiling and I was frightened. She would lie next to me and stroke my brow. She told me to close my eyes and think of pretty things like beautiful dresses and colorful flowers. I find myself repeating these utterances of calming love. I tell her to close her eyes and picture pretty things, happy things. She seems to be at peace. I don't think she feels distress. I am not sure if she realizes the gravity of her situation. I hope that she doesn't, but she is not a stupid person. We have been with her a long time. She knows we must be tired. Forever the mother, she motions for us to go home to rest. I tell her not now. Maybe later. It is five a.m., and I've been up for twenty-four hours, twelve at her side. She has been quiet, restful, peaceful, stable. I am overcome by exhaustion. Todd, my oldest son with daughters of his own, comes up to me, rubs my back and whispers, "You're one great daughter." Rosie's assimilation into secular America was countered by Todd's becoming a *ba'al teshuvah* (returnee to Judaism). She talked with him about her religious upbringing and told him how her father, whom she adored and whose positivity she emulated, lived like a *tzaddik* (righteous person), died like a *tzaddik*, and was buried like a *tzaddik*.

Steve insists that I go home. He promises that he will stay with her and make sure she is comfortable. These are my prayers for her not only on *Shabbos* but during the week, too - for her to be comfortable even though she is not well. Steve has always been there for her, intervening just enough to get her back on track. I thank him for keeping her alive for so many years. He says it wasn't him - it was God. I am eternally grateful to both of them.

I am torn. I do not want to leave her. But I can function no longer. I will do her no good exhausted. So I give in, and Jeff, my middle son, takes me home to take a short rest. I cannot sleep. We sit in the living room and talk. Jeff is a good listener. The best. He knows how sad I am about my mother. But I know that he is also concerned about *his* mother. I tell him how I will miss her and that I don't know what I will do without her. He listens sympathetically, without interruption. He reminisces about the special bond he had with his grandmother. At the age of seventy-two, she took her driving test to renew her license which had long since lapsed. Three years later, Jeff got his license and when she bought a new car, she offered to share the car with him. "Now we have wheels, Grandma!" He cheered her with the freshness of youth while she advised him with the wisdom of age.

Restless and anxious to see her, I ask Jeff to take me back to the hospital. When I return to her bedside, Steve tells me she has been resting comfortably. He has been monitoring her closely, non-stop. When he senses that she is in pain, he adjusts her IV or her position or her morphine to alleviate the discomfort. The intensive care doctor, Dr. Melamud, thinks she must be Steve's mother. When he explains he is the son-in-law, the doctor is taken aback. He says she must be a very special woman for a son-in-law to stay with her all night, not leaving her side, even for a moment. Finally, as she looks at Steve for the last time, with a loving smile, she utters her final words:

"Darling. I love you."

* * * * *

January 29, 2001

I will call my mother tomorrow to tell her that I am going to a funeral on Tuesday. Rosie died. "What a nice lady!" I will remind her. "She was always such an inspiration!" But I realize that this is crazy - it is *her* funeral. How can that be?

I will miss her more than I can imagine. I will have to draw on the thousands of conversations I have had with her in the past in order to cope without her in the future.

After I became an adult, I was just as inexorably attached to my mother as I had been as a young child, deriving spiritual and emotional sustenance from a physically weak but emotionally strong and loving mother. Is the bond ever broken? I do not believe it ever will be. The song is sung; the words are spoken; the feeling is felt. The emotions are overwhelming!

TWO

THE EULOGIES

MINE. . . .

My mother was a survivor. Even though her hands and feet were gnarled and deformed with severe arthritis and her bones and joints were too weak to support her body, her spirit was strong and she was an inspiration to others whom some might think were more fortunate than she. Her proverbial cup was always half full, never half empty. She was positive and optimistic, seeing the good in people and in life itself. She gave strength to people much stronger than she, advice to those more educated, tips on love and marriage to many who were half or even one-quarter her age.

It was my mother's patience and kindness that I remember most, second only to her loyalty to her husband and protection and unconditional love for her children. "Hurt me," she would say "but not my child." When my second grade teacher, Miss Goodman, accused me of being a thief because I had taken home my reading book so I could proudly show my mother how well I could read, my mother dropped what she was doing in the cleaning store, grabbed my hand, ran down the subway stairs, and rushed with me to Macy's on Herald Square to buy me the identical book so I would have my very own to read.

When we were sick, my mother taught us how to play pinochle and spent hours playing with us. Before the age of eight, I knew about melding, suits, pinochles, marriages, points, and the value of the Jack of Diamonds and Queen of Spades. For every cup of tea she cajoled us into drinking, she gave us a nickel (inflation raised this amount to a quarter when her grandchildren came along).

She painstakingly taught me how to figure out the value of "x" in algebra problems and how to complete geometry proofs (and never got angry). Even when I was in kindergarten, she never lost her patience when I repeatedly spelled "cat" "dee oh gee." She barely ever lost her temper. She exuded a genuine sweetness to people. "Remember," she would say, "you catch more flies with honey than with vinegar."

Despite poor vision, she always saw the good; unable to stand, she stood firm in her convictions; pain and suffering didn't detract from her compassion for others; difficulty in breathing never removed her radiant smile; blindness didn't diminish her eyes from lighting up when she heard good news from someone she loved; and a mechanical device that made her heart beat didn't take away the humanity, compassion and warmth of heart she had for others.

At one of our weekly *Parsha* (Torah portion) classes, the rabbi was asked about life support. He said that we all have a soul and we were put on earth to fulfill a task assigned by God. "Who's to say," he asked, "when a person has completed the task assigned to him?" My mother completed many tasks. She provided a model for successful child-rearing and being a loving mother. She taught us the ingredients for a happy marriage consisting of mutual love and respect. She provided inspiration to every person she met. She taught through example the power of love and faith in overcoming inevitable obstacles. She remained calm during times of turmoil and mustered up strength in times of overwhelming difficulties.

She was a firm believer that no one is born a minute before his time nor dies a minute after his time. Until twenty-four hours before her time came, I was still calling my mother as I always had to hear her cheerful and reassuring voice, to share our thoughts, to ask her advice. When I returned home from the hospital at five o'clock on that morning after saying my final good-bye and giving her one last kiss, I said to myself, "I'll call Mommy later and tell her I have to go to a funeral on Tuesday." Oh, no. I won't. I can't. It is *her* funeral.

In my heart, she will never be gone. She will be here with me and for me forever.

* * * * *

STEVE'S. . . .

At the conclusion of each of the Five Books of the Torah, it is customary to proclaim,

"Be strong! Be strong! And may we be strengthened!"

Be strong . . . Be strong . . . And may we be strengthened.

Strength . . . Strength characterized by a non-stop giving, caring, and loving, while maintaining a positive cheerful outlook in the face of her painful, progressive, crippling ailments.

When I first met Rosie over forty years ago, she already had advanced psoriatic rheumatoid arthritis. It should have subsided, but that was not to be. All the while I knew her, she was always concerned about everyone, there to help in any way she could, whether with kind words, advice, or generosity.

She befriended everyone. Loved those close to her. Rosie saw the cup half full. Her eyes sparkled in gratitude for any kindness or joy that came to her or to others. Rosie saw the full half of the cup.

As her life unfolded, she wished she could hold this pot . . . this dish . . . the cards . . . her great-grandchildren.

She wished her feet were better . . . her knee . . . her hip . . . her walking . . . that she could stand . . . turn over in bed.

She wished she could see the road . . . the cards . . . the faces of her grandchildren.

Tired . . . A pacemaker to go with her artificial wrist, knee, and hip.

Acute shortness of breath . . . Lasix for her heart failure.

More difficulty in breathing . . . an aerosol and treatments with a breathing machine for her chronic obstructive pulmonary disease.

Excruciating back pains . . . her aortic aneurysm dissecting . . . morphine.

Except for "I love you," the last thing she said was, "Steve, tell the nurse I can't see."

I didn't. I told her that she was blind.

Rosie saw. Rosie understood. Rosie knew.

"Be strong! Be strong! And may we be strengthened!"

THREE

ROSIE AND ME

"Say not in grief 'he is no more',
but live in thankfulness that he was."
(Hebrew Proverb)

February 11, 2001

It has been sixteen days since my mother's death. I have been thinking of her continually during this time. I see her as I always had seen her, sitting up in her wheelchair by the dining room table eagerly awaiting my arrival or dozing in her large mechanical chair that lifted her up, reclined with pillows under her back and head, her legs and feet covered with a collection of hand-crocheted blankets. When she was feeling especially weak, I found her in her hospital bed, lying on her left side facing the television set she could no longer see and the window open to the bushes and grass she was no longer able to admire. Blindness sharpened her other senses. She followed television programs solely through hearing, and she relished feeling the brisk cold wind coming through the window during the winter and the balmy breezes in the summertime. In autumn and spring, rain or snow, the window was always open so that she could feel the cool breeze and smell the fresh air.

I have been reflecting about her final years when, unable to support her own body weight, she could no longer stand. She was confined to a wheelchair and had to wear diapers. She relied on others to read her mail because macular degeneration blinded her. Depletion of calcium in her bones, along with joints that were not only inflamed but also severely deformed, prevented her from turning in bed, from finding a comfortable position unless pushed, pulled, lifted, or as she would say, "shlepped" by someone else. Years earlier, Rosie joked with my father that you would need a derrick to lift her.

Her room was filled with all the paraphernalia necessary for someone who was chronically ill. There was a large contraption called a Hoyer Lift sitting in the corner of her bedroom in case she ever needed to be hoisted in and out of bed. It was positioned next to the giant oxygen machine where packages of Dignity diapers were piled. I took solace in the fact that my mother could not see the indignity that her illness had wrought upon her. She could not turn on the television, adjust the volume, or change the channel. She used a bell to call for someone to bring her water, unwrap a Hall's menthol cough drop and place it in her mouth, adjust her pillow, move her on her side, cover her perpetually cold feet, open the window or close it, give her a breathing treatment, dial the phone to call one of her children, lift her onto the commode, take her off the commode, change her diaper, clean up her mess, change the sheet, put salve on her sore feet, apply one cream to her psoriasis, another to the bed sores on her buttocks. Dignity! *What* dignity? Robbed of her physical dignity, she clung to her self-respect. She rarely complained.

No matter where or in what position I found my mother, I was always greeted by her wonderful smile. We had practically the same conversation during each visit. We talked about the children, the grandchildren, and the great-grandchildren, what was new, how *they* were doing, how *I* was doing, how *she* was doing. She was always doing fine!

She tells me about her neighbors - who died, who had a stroke, who was away on vacation, who moved, who was taken to a nursing home. We talked about dreams and their corresponding numbers contained in her home health aide's "Dream Book" that she played in the lottery - boxed, wheeled and straight, similar to the betting at the race track. And there were other dreams not number-related. She dreamt that she was running away from someone trying to kidnap her from her elementary school P.S. 188. Once she dreamt that her mother was summoning her. Often she dreamt that she was dancing or walking and seeing again.

A week before she died, I brought Rosie CDs and a CD player. We laughed together at old Burns and Allen radio shows and sang along with the Yiddish songs. I was only able to hum the tunes and struggled to read the transliteration of the titles of the songs, but Rosie was able to effortlessly rattle off the titles in perfect Yiddish; and without changing the sweet contented smile on her face, she translated the words for me.

During one of our last visits together, she was lying on her side, her back already hurting. Was this the start of the aneurysm slowly, insidiously, unmercifully dissecting which would lead to her demise less than a week later? I stood over her, massaging her back to relieve the discomfort which had not yet become intolerable.

I never hesitated to tell my mother how much I loved her. So many adult children do not verbalize their love for their parents. I would be flabbergasted when I witnessed an adult daughter reprimanding her mother for not walking fast enough, for not understanding what she was saying, or for taking up so much of her time bringing her to the doctor or the dentist for an appointment. I was neither self-conscious nor embarrassed to express my feelings of love for my mother. They poured out from my heart. I let her know what a great mother she was and how I tried to emulate her in my own role as wife, mother and grandmother. I could tell that she felt flattered, and I felt so fortunate to embody her attributes that I so admired.

Although my grasp of Yiddish is limited, I find myself using the same expressions she used. I address my children with "*Mein leiben, mein lechtes*" ("my love, my life"); and I hear Rosie's voice when I tell them: "*Zah nicht kein yolt*" ("Don't be a fool)"; "*Zog dos nicht*" ("Don't worry)"; "*Luzze ge macht*" ("Let him be"); "*Gut, shrek mir* but *struf mir nicht*" ("God, frighten me but don't punish me"); "*The mensch tracht and Gut lacht*" ("The people make plans and God laughs)". "*A bee gissint*" ("As long as you're well"); "*Ich chub nicht kain koyich*" ("I have no strength"); *Kim a hea*" ("Come here"); "*Shra nicht*" ("Don't yell"); "*Vous machsta*" ("How do you feel); "*Vous vilsta*" ("What do you want"); "*Zah gissint*" ("Be well").

I asked my mother to give me Yiddish lessons, and a few months before she died, I brought over a book of Yiddish words and expressions. We laughed as I stumbled over the transliteration of "*Foxen zolsta vi a tsibbila mit en cup in drert*" ("You should grow like an onion with your head in the earth").

Mom, "*Uch deer emes lieb*" (I truly love you).

* * * * *

June 25, 2001

The craving is insatiable. I don't know how to satisfy it. I consume four cups of coffee, three slices of bread with apricot preserves, even a piece of the forbidden Halavah, so high in fat and sugar. But nothing helps. I sit outside. I try to read. I work. I rearrange closets. I clean the house and dust the furniture. Nothing is satisfying. Nothing can fill the emptiness I feel. And then it becomes clear. I need her. I want her.

For fifty-six years, she has wished me a happy birthday, and this will be my first birthday ever without her - the first time I won't hear her lovely off-key rendition of *Happy Birthday,* always the first call on the morning of my birthday.

Sometimes, when I bemoan how much I miss my mother, I feel very selfish. Women I know personally have lost their mothers at much younger ages. Some were young adults; others were only children - one at sixteen, at twelve, even at eight years old. So I consider myself very fortunate to have had her for so many years. How many grandmothers, like me, still have their mothers? How many are able to link the generations, exchanging ideas about what was then and what is now? But it does not diminish how much I miss her and wish she were here to wish her baby, her *ketzila*, a happy birthday.

I find myself fading in and out of the stark reality and painful truth that she is no longer here, that I can never again call her on the telephone, visit her, laugh with her, talk to her, kiss her, hug her, touch her. Surely, I know intellectually that she has died. I was with her when she took her final breath, held her still and lifeless hand as she passed from this world to the next, gave a eulogy, witnessed the lowering of the plain pine coffin into the ground, joined my fellow mourners in the Jewish custom of filling the grave with dirt one shovelful at a time, paid the funeral director, made copies of her death certificate, and opened a checking account "*The Estate of Rose Anderman*". So how can I not know that she has passed away? Why, then, do I plan to call her, to visit her, to bring her the food she likes to eat? It is the emotional consciousness that refuses to accept her physical absence.

PART EIGHT

ROSIE'S LEGACY

ONE

ROSIE'S FIRST NAMESAKE
March 4, 2001

Aviva *Raisl* was born at 6:12 a.m. on March 4, 2001, exactly thirty-four days after the person for whom she was named passed away. She entered this world reluctantly - just as her great grandmother left this world reluctantly. Did their souls pass each other, each on her way to where the other had dwelled? Did my mother say, "*Ketzila* (little kitten), now it is your turn - be strong, be kind, be good - *Zahgazunt* (Be well)!" Did the newcomer respond, "I will. I will carry your name proudly."

It took my daughter, Emily, four hours of almost continual pushing to get Aviva *Raisl* to leave her dwelling of nine months. With great trepidation, she approached but then retreated back to the comfort and security of the only world she had ever known. Emily wanted the baby **out** while the baby wanted to stay where she was, creating a four-hour tug-of-war, ultimately won, as it always is, by the mother!

A month earlier, a similar tug-of-war in reverse was unfolding. Rosie tried desperately not to leave the only world she had known for eighty-seven years. But the next life was calling, and she could hold on no longer. She relinquished the heavy rope, exhausted and completely spent. Death had won. It always does.

TWO

THE UNBROKEN CHAIN

Every moment of our lives presents us with a new experience. There are thousands, perhaps millions of possible experiences. Which ones do we remember?

Lately, I have been thinking that those that are most memorable are the "firsts" and the "lasts". What contrasts there are!

I am sitting in my garden rocking Emily's first born, Aviva *Raisl* ("Rosie") in the carriage, lulling her to sleep. How vivid in my mind is her first breath, no scream - just the first breath - watching as her bluish-gray color slowly changes to pink. The joy and exhilaration are indescribable. Welcome to the world! So many experiences to look forward to - most to enjoy, some less so. What a contrast to the one after whom she is named - the final breath of Rosie. I watched for hours, each dying breath, kept regular by morphine and a pacemaker - until the final one. Also no fanfare. No screaming or flailing. Just the last, the final breath. The similarity of the peacefulness in these breaths contrasts with the emotions they evoke. The first breath makes us feel hope and anticipation. The last breath leaves us in utter despair and resignation. However, it is the similarity of these two breaths that leaves me hopeful. There is an acceptance of changing places; and Rosie's acceptance of things that cannot be changed has been passed on to my new granddaughter, Aviva *Raisl*.

I clearly remember Emily, my long-awaited girl, sleeping on my stomach as I sang to her the tune of Barbra Streisand's hit song, *Jenny Rebecca, Four Days Old.* I looked at this beautiful miracle and made up my own song for her: *"Emily Jill, four hours old, how do you like the world so far?"* What an impact these first experiences that can never be duplicated have on us!

Aviva *Raisl* is awake. Back to her firsts! And the drastic contrasts to the lasts of the Rosie for whom she is named.

The first time I saw her - and the last time I saw her. The first song, the first embrace, the first kiss, the first feeding; the first smile, the first - that ever-exciting first. And the last of each of these - the very last.

* * * * *

I have received Rosie's final bills from AT&T, PSE&G, Allstate. Final! Everything is so final. Her final days. It's the final curtain. That is what makes the death of a loved one so painful. It is so damn final. There is no turning back.

THREE

ROSIE'S WORDS OF WISDOM

"*Got shrek mir,* but *shtrof mir nischt.*" ("God frighten me, but don't punish me"). These words echoed in my mind as I sat in the "Quiet Room" of Fox Chase Cancer Center, while my husband was undergoing a long and tedious surgery for prostate cancer.

Who could know that her words would resonate with me eight years after she died. But all of Rosie's words of wisdom are timeless and stay with me each and every day.

So when Steve was diagnosed with cancer, I realized that God had *shreked* (frightened) us but hoped he would not *shtrof* (punish) us. Sitting in the "Quiet Room" on what would have been my father's 98th birthday, I concentrated on my mother's reassuring smile, reflecting on the comfort I had always gotten from her.

I heard her voice in my head, "Don't worry, *Ketzila.* He will be okay." I clung to her words as I sat in the room filled with bibles of every religion set aside for family members to meditate while their loved ones were undergoing the biggest medical challenge of their lives. And sure enough, everything turned out okay.

116

It is a phrase I use often, always praying for a good outcome. When I had chest pain, jaw pain, sweating, and shortness of breath, I was lucky. It turned out not to be a heart attack. Once again, I thought to myself that God had frightened me, but He didn't punish me.

"When they're little, they step on your toes. When they're big, they step on your heart." They make a mess when they try to help; they spill their milk; they get crumbs all over the floor; they flood the kitchen when they wash the dishes; they scratch the fender when they try to park the car. When they are older, they can disappoint you in ways that break your heart. Some children hang out with the wrong friends, contract terrible diseases, or find themselves in financial difficulty. Others might ignore you or, worse, merely tolerate you. The toes or the heart? Which is better to be stepped upon? The choice is clear.

"The most important person in your life is your mate. Then come your children. And after that, your parents." Rosie always put her husband before all others. If I invited her to dinner, her response was always, "I'll ask Daddy." Once she created an uproar when she declined an invitation to a family birthday party so her *Shimshee* wouldn't miss his bowling night. Rosie did not care about any repercussions. Simon came first. He always did. She defended him to the end. There was no question.

117

I have emulated this in my own marriage of over fifty years, and I have tried to teach my own married children the same lesson. Rosie was right, as usual. When all is said and done, it is your mate who is always there, both physically and emotionally, when you are in need or when you are not. He is the one I can always count on, the person always in my corner, the pillar of my existence.

"If you smoke, smoke your own. If you drink, drink your own." Although I smoked occasionally, I am not aware that my mother knew; and I did not believe that she thought I drank. Yet her admonition was clearly stated to me anytime I was about to place myself in a situation where drinking and smoking might occur. She warned me that someone might spike my drink or give me a cigarette that contained something other than tobacco. I would listen patiently, smiling to myself, but heeded her warning nonetheless.

"When God gave out brains, you were at the front of the line" (as our chests swelled with pride); *"but then God said, 'A...BOUT face'!"* Rosie gave her children unconditional love but refused to give unconditional, undeserved praise. She never failed to compliment us for our accomplishments, but neither would she automatically tell us how great we were. Unlike many parents today, as well as Little League coaches who give everyone, winners and losers alike, a trophy, she never gave us a false sense of

accomplishment when we fell short of her expectations. Not a wealthy woman, she encouraged us in our endeavors with, "I've got my money on you!" A humble person by nature, she was careful to keep our egos in check, so when our chests swelled because Rosie implied that we were at the front of the line, she made sure our egos didn't get too big by telling us what God said next!

Rosie empathized and related to everyone - young and old alike. She often said, *"The problems of a two-year-old are just as serious to him as the problems of a fifteen-year-old, a forty-year-old, a sixty-year-old, or an eighty-year-old are to them. So the angst that a toddler feels when losing his security blanket is just as serious to him as the teenager losing her boyfriend, the forty-year-old losing his job, the sixty-year-old losing his retirement money, or the eighty-year-old losing her independence."*

My mother rarely made what she referred to as "a big *tsimmes* (fuss)" about things. If something was troubling me and I didn't know the solution, she would often say, *"Ketzila, zog dos nischt. Ketzila, don't worry. . .so fast my arthritis should heal up."* She put things in the order of their priority and put a logical and reasonable perspective on everything. Nothing was a big deal. She never belittled anyone else's problems, and she had an uncanny knack for putting a positive spin on seemingly negative situations and placing everything in its proper perspective. If the roof leaked or if a tree fell on the fence, she minimized my over-reaction, "*Carola,*" she said. "*It's only money; and with money you get honey.*" If I was not sure if a particular plan I had was going to come to fruition, she often said, "*Yeah, yeah. Nischt, nischt.*" If it happens, fine. If not, well that's okay, too. And if I got upset over what someone said or did, she would uncharacteristically blurt out, "*Carola. It's a bunch of shit!*"

She refused to allow anything to shock or catch her off guard. A fatalist, one of her favorite sayings was *Az mo leit, derleit me alas* (If you live long enough, you will live to see everything).

PART NINE

MOVING ON

ONE

A SPACE FOR ROSIE

On her seventy-fifth birthday, I drove my mother to the cemetery to visit my father. He died six-and-a-half months before their fiftieth wedding anniversary. No gold mementos to celebrate. My father lies to the left of my mother's empty plot. To the right is a doctor whose loose dirt shows that he has just arrived. According to the foot stone, he was born three days after my father but lived three years longer. I wonder if he got to celebrate his fiftieth anniversary.

"I'm glad there's a doctor next to me," my mother exclaims, "in case I don't feel so good!"

I tell her she better lose some weight because her plot is pretty narrow. Without missing a beat, she retorts, "It's okay. I like to sleep on my side anyway, so there will be enough room!"

So now, almost twelve years after visiting the cemetery, Rosie is resting between the love of her life, her *Shimshee*, and the doctor she never met.

TWO

THE VOID
March 22, 2001

My head is bursting with things I want to tell her. Your great-grandchildren are adorable. Sarah, at three, boasts that she wears "unnerwear" (underwear). She wants to know where Abba's Meermar (her father's grandma - YOU) is. She remembers you well, playing with her as you lay in bed. She loves to play with the toy housecleaning set you got her, consisting of a broom, an apron, and a dust cloth. Nechama is two and does yoga with me, reaching for the sky and doing the downward-facing dog. Chana, the baby, is a "roly-poly" and smiles all the time. Jeff is going to Paris to see his girlfriend. We're going to Pearl and Lenny's surprise fortieth wedding anniversary party. I used Daddy's sewing machine. Poor Stanley Anderman died of colon cancer. Emily is up all night because Aviva *Raisl* is fussy. But, wait! These fleeting urges to call or to visit, to ask advice, to laugh, to reminisce, to commiserate, are instantaneously replaced by the harsh reality. There is no one there to call. Of course. How can there be? Aviva *Raisl* is here. She is named for you.

THREE

THE FIRST *YAHRZEIT*
(Anniversary of her death)
January 30, 2002

*"Death is no more than passing from one room
into another.
But there's a difference for me, you know,
because in that other room I shall be able to see."*

Helen Keller

It is exactly a year since the time I said the final good-bye. My thoughts return me to the room where my mother's coffin, draped with a cloth of blue and white, dominates the surroundings while the *Shomer* (ritual attendant) continues reciting *t'hillim* (psalms) - prayers for the dear departed loved one, who is my mother. We are assured that the *Shomer* maintained the physical aspects of *K'vod HaMet* (the respect and honor of the deceased) and remained in attendance through the night.

I enter with reluctance and trepidation, all so new to me, and I approach her coffin for the first time. I place my hand on top of the blue and white drape, and suddenly, I begin to caress it as I had caressed my mother so

125

many times in her lifetime. Gently moving my hand over the draped coffin, my mind transcends time and place. I feel a small smile form on my lips as I close my eyes and see my mother, perhaps in Heaven, smiling and walking, yes walking, with none of the physical barriers that prevented her from walking for so many years on this earth. Her hands are straight with beautiful long fingers (*"piano player's fingers"*, as she would often say while admiring the fingers of a new baby), and she is energetic, looking for my father. She is carefree and free - freed from pain, free from the confines of her wheelchair, free from the dependency of others to perform her most private and personal functions - freed from medications, exhaustion, fear, the smells and indignity of sickness and loss of control of bodily functions. She is walking and running, just as she had described to me in one of her dreams. She is happy, unquestionably, she is very happy.

She sees my father and cries out with joy,
"See that man. That's the man I married!"

* * * * *

My eyes close, my hand moving in circular motions, massaging the coffin as though it were her, reminding me of when I was a little girl and she would ask me to massage her aching back, unable and not wanting to stop. I am immersed in the vision of my mother, unaware of my surroundings, experiencing the joy I feel seeing her so unfettered and free. Any trepidation and reluctance that I might have had when I first approached her coffin are gone.

I realize that the rabbi has entered the room. My eyes open and, just as one needs to adjust to the light and surroundings when awakening from a deep sleep, I abruptly come back to reality. My mother has died; it is her funeral; she is soon to be buried; and I am overcome with sadness.

The rabbi has asked my siblings and me - the children of the "deceased" - to join him by the coffin. I am already there, having traveled with my mother beyond time and space to what she and I secretly now know is a better place for her. In this, I take great comfort.

The rabbi, patient, kind, and filled with compassion, recites the prayer for the dead and, to preserve my modesty, asks a female member of the *Chevra Kadisha* (Burial Society of the synagogue) to rip my blouse as a symbol - the rending of my garment reflecting my grief. It symbolizes the tearing of my heart, which is already broken.

The service is concluded, the eulogies are tearfully given, and we embark to the cemetery for her final departure from this world. Appropriately, it is a rainy day. Even the heavens are weeping.

When the last shovel of soil is tossed on top of my mother's coffin, I realize that both Steven and Grandma were right so many years ago when they were both care-free and happy with so much life to hope for and so many happy years to look forward to.

* * * * *

"Grandma, what happens when you die?" asked the innocent little boy.

"You get buried in the ground". . .and

"You go to Heaven."

"*God grant me the serenity*
To accept the things I cannot
change;
Courage to change the things I can;
And Wisdom to know
the difference."

Reinhold Neibuhr
(theologian)

EPILOGUE

The inscription on the tombstone is fading. I try to retrieve the words of love and remembrance, but I cannot. I rub the stone to buff the letters into clarity, but they fade even more. I try some dye, but this only makes it worse and further obliterates the message.

The dream is so real. I do not awaken, so engrossed am I in the effort to clarify the message. I try so hard, but to no avail.

They are playing *Ramblin' Rose* and *Movin' On* on the radio. More signs - new messages.

I hear her calling to me, *"Carola. It is time."*

"Time for what?" I desperately ask.

"Time to move on, Ketzila. Time for you to shed the pain of the fresh, raw wound and to replace it with the wonderful loving memories of the times we shared together."

I quote her every day. Her words of wisdom and encouragement come to me in times of need. What would she say in this situation? How would she handle this controversy? But she has sent me a message. Let the pain subside.

"Remember me, Ketzila, and be happy!"

POST SCRIPT

"Strength does not come from physical capacity. It comes from an indomitable spirit."

Mahatma Gandhi

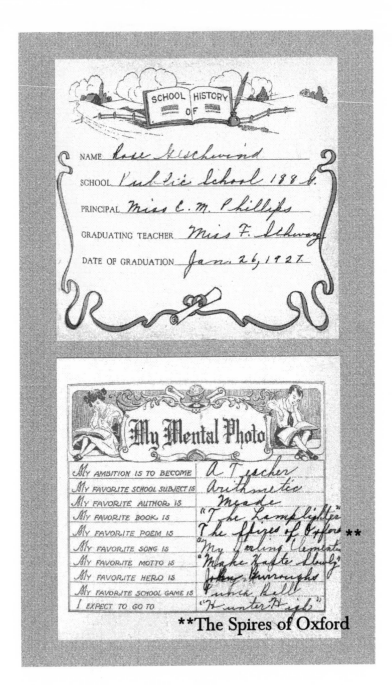

**The Spires of Oxford

The Spires of Oxford
By Winifred M.Letts

I saw the spires of Oxford
    As I was passing by,
The gray spires of Oxford
    Against the pearl-gray sky.
  My heart was with the Oxford men
    Who went abroad to die.

The years go fast in Oxford,
    The golden years and gay,
The hoary Colleges look down
    On careless boys at play.
  But when the bugles sounded war
    They put their games away.

They left the peaceful river,
The cricket-field, the quad,
The shaven lawns of Oxford,
    To seek a bloody sod -
They gave their merry youth away
    For country and for God.

God rest you, happy gentlemen,
    Who laid your good lives down,
Who took the khaki and the gun
    Instead of cap and gown.

God bring you to a fairer place
    Than even Oxford town.

I can't help wondering what prompted Rosie at the innocent age of fourteen to write in her eighth-grade autograph album that *The Spires of Oxford* was her favorite poem. Written in 1916, it tells of the sacrifice young men made when they gave up their carefree lives to go off to war. They relinquished their comfortable lives for a higher cause. Could she have foreseen the fate that would befall her? Clearly, she empathized with "the Oxford men who went abroad to die." Metaphorically, she gave up her "golden years" and "gave [her] merry youth away" to chronic illness; but unlike the "careless boys at play," she did so with neither forethought nor intent. She just got dealt a lousy hand. Instead, those "happy gentlemen" knowingly and intentionally gave up their comfortable lives to face a dreaded outcome.

The brand of empathy she felt for these young boys and the gallantry she saw in them carried her through the obstacles she encountered during her life. Like them, she fought to survive and was an unassuming hero while demonstrating her own brand of bravery.

ACKNOWLEDGEMENTS

This memoir is a labor of love based on decades of journal entries and reflections.

First and foremost, I would like to thank my husband, Steve. Through the years, he has unfailingly encouraged me to complete this memoir. He has patiently read and re-read the manuscript, each time with a fresh eye, and has given me excellent suggestions on how to best tell Rosie's story. He has been my partner, my pillar and my best friend for more than fifty years. I am indebted to my dear mother-in-law, Henrietta Harkavy, for her love and for sharing her wonderful son with me.

My children, Rabbi Chaim (Todd) Harkavy, Jeff Harkavy, and Emily Lerman, gave me invaluable insight into Rosie's relationship with them; and now that the memoir is finally in print, they are freed from my threat that they might have to publish *ROSIE* posthumously!

Writers themselves, my sons offered me advice on flow and structure; and my daughter Emily, an accomplished book editor, painstakingly read, reviewed, and edited several drafts of the manuscript.

I am grateful to Stefani Milan, a budding young author of *The Secret of Kolney Hatch*, for her great help and guidance in bringing this memoir to publication.

I would like to give special thanks to the following people for their encouragement and suggestions in the development of the manuscript: Marlene Alexoff, Debbie Drachman, Denise Harkavy, Stefani Milan, Roseanne Milanese, Renee Robbins, Anita Rosner, and Judy Mulry Silverman.

I am grateful to Carol Sweeney, a talented photo restorer, for helping me with the cover for the book.

I would especially like to thank Rosie's first namesake and my granddaughter, Aviva *Raisl* Lerman. In addition to her persistent encouragement to tell her great-grandmother's story, she has become my marketing advisor and publicist.

I would like to thank my siblings Pearl and Siggy for being there with me while we all experienced the joy of having Rosie for our mother.

Last, but certainly not least, I would like to thank my mother, ROSIE . . . the inspiration for this memoir.

ABOUT THE AUTHOR

Carol Harkavy was born in New York City a year before the end of World War II. She grew up on Sixteenth Street in Greenwich Village. In 1955, her family moved to Spring Valley, New York, a rural town thirty-five miles north of New York City. She attended The City College of New York, where she later became a tenured instructor in the Speech Department. After marrying her high school sweetheart, she moved to Cincinnati, Ohio, where she received her Master of Arts degree. Writing has always been her passion, and she has kept journals all of her life. It was those journal entries that acted as a foundation upon which *Rosie* was built.

Made in the USA
Middletown, DE
13 February 2019